THE
Motherhood
MANIFESTO

WHAT AMERICA'S MOMS WANT

AND WHAT TO DO ABOUT IT

Joan Blades *and*
Kristin Rowe-Finkbeiner

Nation Books
New York

ALSO BY JOAN BLADES

Mediate Your Divorce:
A Guide to Cooperative Custody, Property, and Support Agreements

Joan is also an organizer of and a contributor to MoveOn.org's
50 Ways to Love Your Country:
How to Find Your Political Voice and Be a Catalyst for Change.

ALSO BY KRISTIN ROWE-FINKBEINER

The F-Word: Feminism In Jeopardy—
Women, Politics and the Future

Kristin is also a contributor to
The Essential Hip Mama:
Writing from the Cutting Edge of Parenting

With deep appreciation and love for our Mothers,
and for all Mothers.

THE MOTHERHOOD MANIFESTO

Published by
Nation Books
An Imprint of Avalon Publishing Group, Inc.
245 West 17th St., 11th Floor
New York, NY 10011

Nation Books is a co-publishing venture of the Nation Institute and Avalon
Publishing Group, Incorporated.

In order to protect the privacy of some interviewees, some names have been
changed.

Library of Congress Cataloging-in-Publication Data is available.

ISBN: 1-56025-884-5
ISBN-13: 1-56025-884-1

9 8 7 6 5 4 3 2

Book design by Maria E. Torres
Printed in the United States of America
Distributed by Publishers Group West

Contents

Acknowledgments

We're deeply grateful to be part of a much larger community—mothers, workers, activists, academics, employers, fathers, researchers, and leaders—who infused this book with heart and soul. We are utterly indebted to them.

We particularly thank: Katie Bethell, Mary Bond, Wes Boyd, Carl Bromley, Bill Finkbeiner, Anne Mathews, Leslie Miller, and Todd Schuster.

This book wouldn't have been written without the women and men who shared their expertise, ideas, and experiences. Here's a partial list: Selena Allen, Liz Banse, Helen Blank, Shelley Waters Boots, Heather Boushey, Ellen Bravo, Lori Brennick, Alison Buist, Anna Burger, Amy Caiazza, Tim Collings, Vicki Conrad, Shelley Correll, Ann Crittenden, Yasmine Daniel, Diane Devoy, Sharon Dorsett, Ann Eastman, Jack Eastman, Susan Eixenberger, Danny Feingold, Kim Finkbeiner, Netsy Firestein, Ellen Galinsky, Kim Gandy, Gina Glantz, Jessica Goodheart, John de Graaf, Jodi Grant, Lucas Grohn, Jacob S. Hacker, Matthew Hendel, Christina Henry, Irma Herrera, Lorri Holland, Lettecia Ives, Madeline Janis-Aparicio, Jim Johnson, Bree Johnston, Vicky Lovell, Don Mayer, Martha Mendillo, Marsha Meyer, Wendy McKinney, Donna Norton,

Alfreda Oxley, Kiki Peppard, Marcie Pitt-Catsouphes, Steven Pitts, Liz Perle, Miriam Peskowitz, Michelle Presnell, Deb Richter, Patricia Q. Schoeni, Karen Schulman, Brynn Seibert, Josh Silver, Mindy Standering, Judith Statdman-Tucker, Jenny Stone, Angenita Tanner, Betsy Taylor, Amelia Warren Tyagi, Jane Waldfogel, Elizabeth Warren, and Joan Williams.

Not to forget the multitude of colleagues, friends, and family that read a chapter, connected us with resources, helped us think through a concept, weighed in on the title, and encouraged us in a host of ways. Thank you!

We also send a special thank you to our children Robin, Alec, Connor, and Anna for putting up with us while we wrote this book, as well as to our husbands, Wes and Bill.

1

Motherhood in America

Life, Liberty, Parenthood, and the Pursuit of Happiness

In the deep quiet of a still dark morning Renee reaches her arm out from under her thick flowered comforter and across the bed to hit the snooze button on her alarm clock. For a few blessed (and pre-planned) minutes she avoids the wakeful classic rock blaring into her bedroom from her alarm. Renee hits the snooze button exactly three times before finally casting off her covers. She does this each morning, and each morning she sleepily thinks the same thing, "It's too early. I was just at work two seconds ago, and I don't want to go back already."

Everything about Renee's morning is structured for speed and efficiency. At 5:45 A.M., with her young son, Wade, and husband, Alan, still sleeping, Renee drags herself out of bed and sleep-walks to the shower. She brushes her teeth while the shower is warming, making sweeping circles on the mirror with her hand so she can see her reflection. Renee's movements, though she's thoroughly tired, are crisp, hurried, and automatic—she's repeated the routine daily for several years.

Renee knows exactly how long each of her morning tasks will take to the minute. That, for instance, between 6:00 A.M. and 6:12 A.M. she needs to put on her makeup, get herself dressed, get her son's clothes out and ready for the day, and get downstairs to the kitchen to start breakfast.

All this is done with an eye on the clock and a subtle, yet con-stant, worry about time, "I'm always worried that I'm going to be late to work." Her mind loops over the potential delays that could be ahead, "Is there going to be traffic? Am I going to get stuck behind a school bus? Is my son going to act normal when I drop him off or is he going to be stuck to my leg? Am I going to get a parking space in the office garage or am I going to have to run five blocks through the city to get to work on time?" And if there isn't any garage parking, which happens often, then in order to be on time to work Renee has to run up six flights of stairs in heels because she doesn't have extra time to waste waiting for an elevator. She's done this climb more than once.

Why the stress? At her work, if Renee is late more than six times, then she's in danger of losing her job. Like many American mothers, Renee needs her income to help provide for her family.

In our modern economy, where more often than not two wage earners are needed to support a family, American women now make up 46 percent of the entire paid labor force.[1] In fact, a study released in June of 2005 found that in order to maintain income levels, parents have to work more hours—two parent families are spending 16 percent more time at work or 500 more hours a year than in 1979 just to keep up.[2] Women, and mothers, are in the workplace to stay. Yet public policy and workplace structures have yet to catch up.

For example, the option of flextime would make a world of difference for Renee and her family, "Flextime would make a huge difference in my life because with my job function there are busy days and late days. As long as I'm there 40 hours a week and get my job done, then I don't know why anyone would care. I don't understand why there's such an 8 A.M. to 5 P.M. 'law' in my workplace."

Renee lives for her family. Even with her harried mornings, she always saves time for a fifteen-minute morning cuddle on the couch with her young son, Wade, before they rush out the door. They chat while snuggling and greet the day together.

> **MAJORITY OF AMERICAN WOMEN ARE WORKING MOMS**
>
> When Renee became Wade's mother one hot summer night five years ago, she joined the 82 percent of all American women who become mothers by the time they are forty-four years old.[14]
>
> Women, the majority of whom are moms, are also working more: In the past three decades the percentage of working women has skyrocketed (from 63 percent of twenty-five to thirty-four-year-old women in 1975, to a striking 81 percent in 1999).[15]

WHY THE MOST IMPORTANT JOB IN THE WORLD IS STILL THE LEAST VALUED

by Ann Crittenden, author of *The Price of Motherhood*

The most important job, even economists agree, is raising the next generation. This is still predominantly women's work, and they are still unpaid, badly paid, and often disrespected for doing it. Caring for others, especially for children, is so taken for granted, especially in the U.S., that having a baby is the single worst financial decision an American woman can make.

Take jobs. They are designed ideally for people who have no family life—or can delegate the family work to someone else. As a result, after they have children many women either work part-time or leave paid employment altogether. Often this is not their preferred choice; it's a path they are forced to take because of workplace rigidities. And it costs women dearly: a college-educated woman with one child can easily pay a "Mommy tax" (lost lifetime earnings) of $1 million.

Each morning as her husband, Alan, who owns a tiling company, gets going to work, it falls to Renee to drive Wade to daycare on her way to work as a payroll specialist at a large bank. It's Renee's job that provides the health insurance and other benefits for her family since her husband owns his own business.

At 7 A.M. sharp Renee and Wade get into the green family Windstar and start driving. Freeway traffic is often stop-and-go during the morning commute, and Renee regularly finds herself sitting in traffic with white knuckles worrying about being late to work. "I have to wake up, wake my kid up, deal with a morning tantrum, drop him off at daycare, fight traffic, agonize about whether I am a horrible mother for leaving him at daycare, worry

Married mothers also soon discover that marriage is not an equal financial partnership. The typical American mother is economically dependent on her spouse, and has no claim on his income in the event of divorce. She and the children face a serious risk of poverty if the marriage ends—a risk that most fathers don't face.

Social policy does little to insure these risks or reward mothers for their economic contribution. Nannies earn Social Security credits; mothers do not. They earn a zero for every year they spend caring for family members. This means that motherhood is the single biggest risk factor for poverty in old age.

This treatment of mothers is an anachronism. We need to stop sentimentalizing mothers and other caregivers and start according their work the respect and material recognition that it deserves—and earns. I believe that this is the big unfinished business of the women's movement. @ Ann Crittenden, 2005

if I'm going to be late to work—and that's just the morning before my work day starts at 8 A.M.," says Renee.

Seemingly mundane challenges like these, Renee tells us, become overwhelming when coupled with the financial anxieties that face so many families in America. Renee and Alan would like to have a second child, but they worry that they simply can't afford one right now. For them, the high cost of childcare for Wade, lack of flextime at work, and daily expenses, all add up to just a one-child family.

"It's horrible when you are considering whether or not you can ever have another child based on if you will be able to get ahead," comments Renee, "and by no means do we live, or want to live extravagantly: we just want two cars, two kids, and a vacation here and there."

Renee and millions of other parents across the country are seriously struggling to meet the demands of work and parent-hood. Vast numbers of women are chronically tired and drained. But the American credo teaches us to be fierce individualists, with the result that most parents toil in isolation and can't envi-sion, or don't expect, help. But when this many families are struggling, it's time to recognize we have common problems that can be most constructively addressed through working together to bring about broad and meaningful change in our families, communities, workplaces, and nation.

The Motherhood Manifesto addresses the shared challenges and needs of mothers and families in America.

The Hardest Job You'll Ever Love

Motherhood is perhaps the most important, and most difficult, job on the planet. While we raise our children out of an innate sense of love and nurturing, we also know that raising happy, healthy children who become productive adults is critical to our future well-being as a nation.

But right now, motherhood in America is at a critical junc-ture. As women's roles continue to evolve, more women than ever are in the workforce, and more children than ever are raised in homes without a stay-at-home parent.[3] At the same time, public and private policies that affect parenting and the work-place remain largely unchanged. We have a twenty-first century economy stuck with an outdated industrial-era family support structure. The result is that parents, mothers in particular, are struggling to balance the needs of their children with the demands of the workplace.

Being a mom in America today involves prodigious amounts of work at home and, for most mothers, in outside jobs as well. Specifically, among all of the moms in America, almost three-quarters have jobs outside of their homes.[4] America's mothers are working, and working hard. Then, too, America's mothers are working hard but for less money than men (and less money than women who are not moms). In fact, right now the wage gap between mothers and non-mothers is greater than between women and men—and it's actually getting bigger. Non-mothers with an average age of thirty earn 10 percent less than their male counterparts; mothers earn 27 percent less; and single mothers earn between 34 percent and 44 percent less.[5] "It is well-established that women with children earn less than other women in the United States," writes Jane Waldfogel of Columbia University in *The Journal of Economic Perspectives*. "Even after controlling for differences in characteristics such as education and work experience,

> **THE MATERNAL WALL EQUALS BIG WAGE HITS**
>
> - Non-mothers earn 10 percent less than their male counterparts; mothers earn 27 percent less; and single mothers earn between 44 percent and 34 percent less. [16]
> - The situation for American mothers is increasingly critical: According to the U.S. Census, women's overall wages are dropping compared to men—women lost a cent between 2002 and 2003, and now make 76 cents for every dollar made by men. Much of this wage gap can be attributed to the maternal wall.[17]

researchers typically find a family penalty of 10–15 percent for women with children as compared to women without children."[6]

What this also means is that it's still common for women and men to hold the same job and receive different pay. In fact, women lost a cent between 2002 and 2003, according to the U.S. Census, and now make 76 cents to a man's dollar.[7] Most of these wage hits are coming from moms because the lower wages they receive drag down the overall average pay for all women.

The United States has a serious mommy wage gap. Why? Because, as Waldfogel writes, "The United States does at least as well as other countries in terms of equal pay and equal opportunity legislation, but . . . the United States lags in the area of family policies such as maternity leave and childcare."[8] Studies show this mommy wage gap is directly correlated with our lack of family friendly national policies like paid family leave and subsidized childcare. In countries with these family policies in place, moms don't take such big wage hits.

Speak to mothers across the nation and you will hear that the vast majority of them find they hit an economic "maternal wall" after having children. By all accounts, this wall is why a huge number of professional women leave the workforce, as well as a core reason so many mothers and their children live in poverty. Tragically, statistics from 2001 reveal that in the United States of America—land of opportunity—a full one-quarter of families with children under age six earned less than $25,000 that year.[9]

An income level that is so low most families of four would qualify for food stamps.[10]

But mothers across America are not just crying out for better (or at least fair and equal) pay; they are also yearning to live a life in which they aren't cracking under pressure, a life in which they know that their children will be well cared for, a life in which it's possible to be at home with their son or daughter even just one afternoon a week without worrying about sacrificing a disproportionate amount of their income and benefits—or simply losing their job altogether.

Some would argue mothers just need to find the proper balance between parenting and career. We believe there is more to it than that.

Jobs on the Line

While Renee's story captures the essence of what millions of working American women face each morning; Kiki's daunting experiences simply trying to find a job shows just how deeply rooted, and widely accepted, discriminating against mothers is in our country.

A single mother of two, Kiki moved to a small, one stoplight Pennsylvania town in 1994. She was truly on her own. Her husband had left several years earlier, when her children were two and four years old. Kiki hadn't known how she'd make it as a single parent until her mother, a petite powerhouse and survivor of a World War II Russian gulag, stepped in to help. But when

Kiki's mother passed away a decade later, there was nothing to keep Kiki in the Long Island city where she'd been living. The rapid property tax increases in Kiki's carefully landscaped neighborhood of gorgeous Cape Cod homes were quickly exceeding her economic reach as a single working mother. So Kiki left in search of a smaller city with a lower cost of living.

With this move, Kiki and the kids were alone in a new town that had just two supermarkets and several diners serving a variety of aromatically enticing pork, sauerkraut, and dumpling dishes. It was just the change she wanted. Kiki was able to buy a Dutch Colonial Cape Cod house at the top of a "small mountain" in the Poconos with nearly two acres of land for a fraction of the

---

THE MOMMY WARS

by Miriam Peskowitz, author of *The Truth Behind the Mommy Wars*

The Mommy Wars began as a mid-80's media-fueled debate about whether it was better for moms to continue in the paid workplace or stay home with their kids. Because all moms lack the true support we need, and because our media loves catfights, these Mommy Wars have had a terribly long life. Today, the judgments about motherhood continue unabated, and the topics expand. The Mommy Wars are no longer just about how we work; they're about how we give birth, how we nourish our children with bottles or breasts, use pacifiers, send them to schools or educate them at home, whether we spank or refrain, or the latest, whether we show ourselves to be excellent mothers by toilet training our children very young. There's always some new lifestyle trend report that's meant to separate good mothers from bad.

The problem with the Mommy Wars? All mothers lose.

The Mommy Wars hurt individual moms and make it harder to get price of her old house. It seemed ideal, until she started looking for a job to support her family.

On a hot, humid August day, at an interview for a legal secretary position in a one-story brick building, Kiki sat down in a hard wooden chair to face a middle-aged attorney ensconced behind a mahogany desk. His framed diplomas lined the walls, and legal books filled the shelves behind him. Kiki remembers the attorney clearly, even his general height at 5'10" and the color of his light brown hair. The interaction was significant enough to remain seared in her mind's eye a decade later. "The first question the attorney asked me when I came in for the interview was, 'Are you married?' The second was, 'Do you have children?'"

---

through days that are already difficult enough. By dividing us, the Mommy Wars take our eyes off the prize of social change. Mothers are failing out there—and not at breastfeeding or at raising good kids. We're failing because right now, our society is so ambivalent about motherhood, women and work that it's harder than need be for women to be mothers, and for mothers to be economically independent. Nearly 62 percent of us mothers are no longer in the full-time workplace. As the hours we're expected to work have increased in the last decade, more and more mothers have dropped out of full-time work. There's a huge wage gap for mothers. We're having a hard time getting back into the workplace if we dare to leave for a few years when the kids are young. And we're not finding decent, fairly paid part-time jobs. This means that moms are suffering. It also means that our economy can't get the benefit of our talents and skills, and that affects our nation's well being.

The Mommy Wars? Not helpful, not for individual mothers, not for our country. Let's call 'em over.

It was the eleventh job interview in which she'd been asked the very same questions since moving to Pennsylvania. After answering eleven times that she wasn't married, and that yes indeed, she was a mother of two, Kiki began to understand why her job search was taking so long.

She decided to address the issue head on this time, "I asked him how those questions were relevant to the job, and he said my hourly wage would be determined by my marital and motherhood status." Kiki then asked the next obvious question: "How do you figure out an hourly wage based on these questions?"

His response was as candid as it was horrifying, "He said if you don't have a husband and have children, then I pay less per hour because I have to pay benefits for the entire family." The attorney noted that a married woman's husband usually had health insurance to cover the kids, and since Kiki didn't have a husband, he was very clear that he "didn't want to get stuck with the bill for my children's health coverage."

Kiki started to get angry, "The weather was warm, and it was warm in the office, and then when I got angry it got a lot warmer!"

It was the first time Kiki pushed for an explanation, and she was appalled by the answer. "I said to him, 'You mean to tell me that if I am doing the exact same work, typing the same exact subpoena as a coworker, you're going to pay me less because I have no husband and have kids?' And he very smugly told me, 'Yes, absolutely.' "

He couldn't do that, it was illegal, Kiki wondered, wasn't it? The attorney countered that it was perfectly legal—and as an attorney, he ought to know. He invited Kiki to check out the law herself and then ushered her out the door (without a job, of course).

Furious, Kiki went straight home, her black and silver 1989 Chevy Blazer hugging every curve as she drove up the winding road to her house. She got out of her car, stomped across the crushed stone pathway to her front door, flung her canvas purse on the couch, and called the Pennsylvania Human Relations Commission. She found out that the lawyer was right. The questions were legal, as was paying a single mother less than other applicants. Pennsylvania, like scores of states, does not have state employment laws that protect mothers.

The sad truth is that Kiki isn't struggling alone. Recent Cornell University research by Dr. Shelley Correll confirmed what many American women are finding: Mothers are 44 percent less likely to be hired than non-mothers who have the same résumé, experience, and qualifications; and mothers are offered significantly lower starting pay (study participants offered non-mothers an average of $11,000 more than mothers) for the same job as equally qualified non-mothers.[11] The "maternal wall" is a reality we must address if we value both fair treatment in the workplace and the contributions working mothers make to our economy.

What Moms Really Want

Stories like those of Renee and Kiki, confirm something just isn't right about what we're doing—or not doing—to address the needs of mothers across our nation. Some companies and states are adjusting and innovating with family friendly programs, but such programs are not the norm.[12] Mothers and their families are hurting. We need to open a whole new conversation about motherhood in the twenty-first century by illuminating the universal needs of America's mothers and spelling out concrete solutions that will provide families—whether rich, poor, or middle class—with real relief.

Frankly, we are at a transition point in American history. While most mothers work in this country, we simply don't have sufficient supports in place for parents and families. To suggest that mothers just need to find the proper balance between work and family is to profoundly misunderstand the issue. The truth is that our society hasn't caught up to support the unprecedented diversity of roles modern women take on in a single day. At the heart of the matter is the need for change.

MOMS IN THE WORKFORCE

Mothers need jobs to support their families, and our country needs women in the workforce. According to a *Harvard Business Review* research report, businesses are starting to worry about talent constraints as a potential labor crunch looms: Our population is getting older, and "the number of workers aged thirty-five to forty-five is shrinking," "immigration levels are stable," and women are among the most well educated people in our population, comprising 58 percent of college graduates.[18] Demographic trends alone point to an urgent economic need to address the needs of mothers.

National policies and programs with proven success in other countries—like paid family leave, flexible work options, subsidized childcare and preschool, as well as healthcare coverage for all kids—are largely lacking in America. These problems are deeply interconnected and often overlap: Without paid family leave parents often have to put their infants in extremely expensive or substandard childcare facilities; families with a sick child, inadequate healthcare coverage, and no flexible work options often end up in bankruptcy (indeed illness is one of the top causes of bankruptcy).

On the up side, fixing one of these problems often has numerous positive repercussions. Family friendly workplace policies are becoming more common, drawing more attention and support because companies that do this well are thriving. These companies are thriving because they have lower employee turnover, enhanced productivity and job commitment from employees, and consequently lower recruiting and retraining costs.[13] The good news is there are plenty of workplace success stories, and we can learn from these successes. Our country can change—and together we can launch the movement to see to it that it does.

To spark this deeply important motherhood revolution, we introduce our Manifesto Points, each of which is explored in the subsequent chapters. Specifically, we ask our readers to support:

- **M** = Maternity/Paternity Leave: Paid family leave for all parents after a new child comes into the family.

- **O** = Open Flexible Work: Give parents the ability to structure their work hours and careers in a way that allows them to meet both business and family needs. This includes flexible work hours and locations, part-time work options, as well as the ability to move in and out of the labor force to raise young children without penalties.

- **T** = TV We Choose and Other After School Programs: Give families safe, educational opportunities for children after the school doors close for the day, including: Create a clear and independent universal television rating system for parents with technology that allows them to choose what is showing in their own homes; support quality educational programming for kids; increase access to, and funding for, after-school programs.

- **H** = Healthcare for All Kids: Provide quality, universal healthcare to all children.

- **E** = Excellent Childcare: Quality, affordable childcare should be available to all parents who need it. Childcare providers should be paid at least a living wage and healthcare benefits.

- **R** = Realistic and Fair Wages: Two full-time working parents should be able to earn enough to adequately care for their family. In addition, working mothers must receive equal pay for equal work.

By tackling these interconnected problems together—rather than in isolation—we create a powerful system of support for families. No mother should have to choose between caring for her infant and feeding her children. Working together, we can improve the quality of our lives. And we can make sure our children inherit a world in which they will thrive as adults and future parents. *The Motherhood Manifesto* is a call to action, summoning all Americans—mothers, and all who have mothers—to start a revolution to make motherhood compatible with life, liberty, and the pursuit of happiness.

To get involved go to **www.MotherhoodManifesto.com.**

2

Maternity/ Paternity Leave

S elena, twenty-seven, pushed a shopping cart full of pasta, rice, tortillas, and other basic food staples that she and her family needed for the coming weeks through a big, bulk grocery store. It was her once a month, major shopping trip. Her son, Anthony, then three years old, was home with her husband. A close friend, Vanessa, joined her to shop that night, and they were bantering back and forth as they walked down the grocery store aisles. Selena was thirty-two weeks pregnant and looked like someone had stuck a balloon under her shirt.

A pain started as a nagging stitch, and she turned to her friend

Vanessa and said, "For some reason my stomach is hurting." Selena wasn't that worried though, she wasn't due for at least another six weeks, and it certainly didn't feel like labor to her. She decided the pain would likely just go away, as many strange pinches and pains do during pregnancy, and continued shopping for her family.

Selena and her husband, James, were excited about their soon-to-be new baby. They had carefully worked out their finances to accommodate a second child. Like 61 percent of American families with children, they both worked.[1] Selena and James relied on both of their pay to support their family, and they knew exactly where they stood financially when the new baby arrived. It wasn't guesswork.

LOW INCOME FAMILIES HAVE LEAST LEAVE

Ironically, access to paid family leave is more often available to women in high paying jobs that also have college or other advanced degrees, than those with lower income and education levels who are living closer to the edge of their family budgets.[26] Compounding the issue is the fact that those with lower incomes are significantly less likely to have any paid sick, personal, or vacation time at all, leaving the most fiscally vulnerable segments of our society unprotected.[27]

One night Selena and James sat down together, worked the figures of their monthly incomes, and calculated out to the hour how much time they could afford for Selena to take off from work. James was working in construction at the time, and Selena worked in an administrative capacity at a nonprofit organization.

Together they figured out that if Selena didn't take any paid leave time for prenatal visits or anything else during her pregnancy, then she could use her accrued paid leave from her sick and vacation time for about two and a half weeks of paid leave after the baby was born (which, of course, left her without any paid vacation or sick leave if either she or her children got sick). After those first two weeks, they could afford for Selena to take off another one and a half weeks unpaid, but when that time was up she needed to be back at work bringing home a paycheck.

Selena was better off than many other American women facing similar predicaments. She lives in one of the four out of fifty states (Connecticut, Hawaii, Washington, and Wisconsin) that has laws guaranteeing the flexible use of accrued paid sick or other leave days to care for a new child.[2]

Yet Selena still shares a fairly common experience with new mothers across America—one of financial difficulties and time stretched too thin with the birth of a child. This experience isn't as common in other nations. In fact, the United States is the only industrialized country in the world that doesn't have *paid* leave other than Australia (which does give a full year of guaranteed unpaid leave to all women, compared with the only twelve weeks of unpaid leave given to those who work for companies with more than fifty employees in the U.S.).[3] A full 163 countries give women paid leave with the birth of a child.[4] Fathers often get paid leave in other countries as well—forty-five countries give fathers a right to paid parental leave.[5]

By way of example, our close neighbor to the north, Canada,

FAMILY LEAVE: A DAD'S PERSPECTIVE
by Matthew Hendel

When we had our first son, I was encouraged to take family leave: four weeks off when he was born, and four more weeks when he was two months old after my wife went back to work. During that time, I was the one who changed his diapers, determined when he needed to be fed, put him to sleep for naps, and played with him.

Even when both parents work similar hours, the cultural myth persists that moms know how to care for children, and dads do not. The act of being my son's primary caregiver put me on equal footing with my wife in terms of how we raise him. It helped pull me out of the mindset of asking my wife for everything, and instead relying on my own intuition in how to care for my child.

gives the birth mother fifteen weeks of partial paid leave for physical recovery, and then also gives another thirty-five weeks of partial paid parental leave that has to be taken before the child turns one. These thirty-five weeks of parental leave can be taken by the mother or the father, or can be shared between the two. The pay during the fifty weeks total of leave related to a new child is 55 percent of the average gross salary over the past twenty-six calendar weeks.[6] All in all, there are fifty weeks of partially paid leave available for new Canadian parents to spend with their child.

Sweden, with about a year of paid family leave and some time specifically reserved for fathers, is often used as *the* example of a model policy.[7] Not surprisingly, with this support, Ann Crittenden writes in *The Price of Motherhood,* "Swedish women on average have higher incomes, vis-à-vis men, than women anywhere else in the world."[8] Yes, Sweden has about a full year of paid family leave.

Sadly, few fathers receive any paid time whatsoever when a child is born. Perhaps more insidiously, even when fathers are given leave, we are often discouraged from really taking the time off. Sure, you can be on leave, our companies tell us, as long as you keep up with email and come to important meetings. In my experience, workplace evaluations also ignore time spent with a new family member when considering workload and goal achievement.

Family leave is not a women's issue. Without family leave for fathers, everybody loses: fathers don't get one-on-one time with their children; mothers become overworked and overburdened with parenting decisions; and, most importantly, our children do not receive the full participation of both parents.

America, on the other hand, generally leaves it up to parents to patch together some type of leave on their own. Some states are starting to give more support to new parents, but only one of our fifty states, California, offers paid family leave. The federal government simply doesn't offer a paid family leave program at all. A weighty consequence emerges from this lack of family support. Research reveals that a full 25 percent of "poverty spells," or times when a family's income slips below what is needed for basic living expenses, begin with the birth of a baby.[9]

The morning after her grocery-shopping trip Selena still felt the strange pain under her rib cage. Starting to get worried, she called her OB and set a time to come in to check everything out. The first available appointment was at 3 P.M. that day, so Selena worked through the day at her desk.

The pain started getting worse as she made the forty-five

minute freeway drive to her OB's office, by then "it was a constant terrible pain, but it wasn't coming and going like labor." She finally made it to her destination, but couldn't find parking—she didn't want leave her car in the parking garage because she was worried about the cost of parking adding to her growing stack of bills that were waiting for her at home. So she parked three blocks away and was in tears by the time she reached her OB's office.

To make a long story short, the OB put Selena on a fetal monitor, found out she really was in labor, and then tried unsuccessfully with several different medications to stop the early labor.

Selena's baby boy, Connor, was born six weeks early the next morning.

Their baby was rushed out of the room and up to the Neonatal Intensive Care unit, Selena's husband rushed up with him, and Selena found herself alone in a hospital bed realizing that she was going to go home well before her baby. She had a tough decision to make.

After their son stabilized, Selena's husband James came back down to her room. They had another difficult talk about finances and Selena's leave from work. They couldn't afford for her to take more time off than originally planned, but both wanted Selena to have the most time possible to bond with her son. With her son stable in the hospital, but not knowing how long until he could come home, the choice was between Selena taking time off when he was in the hospital or waiting to take time off when the baby was released from the hospital and could come home. "There was no way we could afford for me to take off more than we planned," recalls Selena.

They made a difficult decision: They decided it would be best if she waited to take time off until the baby came home. So after Selena had the baby on Thursday, she was released from the hospital Friday, and was back at her desk on Monday morning. "It was the hardest two and a half weeks of my life," she says recalling the ache of being away from her newborn son and the rigorous family schedule at that time.

Her days ran on a complex timetable: She'd get up, drop her older son Anthony off at daycare by 8 A.M., and then she'd go to work, taking regular breaks to pump breast milk for her newborn son. Around 1 P.M. she'd leave work early to go visit her son in the hospital before having to pick up her older son, Anthony, at daycare. Often the family would then go back to the hospital again in the evening after dinner so her husband could spend time with their newborn son as well. "I was in tears every day."

During those weeks her supervisor and co-workers were very understanding. Selena shares how they handled her situation, "Thankfully my supervisor sent out an e-mail that said, 'The person that looks like Selena really isn't her, and she really isn't here.' " This was done so people wouldn't give Selena new or difficult projects during that time, "I just did easy, busy work like filing and data entry to clock in hours—all those projects you need to do but never have time to complete. That way if I left the next day, I wouldn't leave any loose ends and I was prepared to leave at a moments notice."

While Selena's workplace of about fifteen staff accommodated her needs in every way open to them, they couldn't afford to offer Selena what she needed most, paid family leave. The fact that in order to make ends meet Selena still had to go to work every day after the premature birth of her son is a dramatic example of the need for a broad paid family leave policy. Selena needed time to focus on her own recovery and that of her family without the worry of financial ruin.

It's not just Selena's family that would see such benefits from paid family leave. "Studies show that parental leave results in better prenatal and postnatal care, more intense parental bonding over a child's lifetime, and lower accident rates in the first year of life. Parental leave policies also increase the likelihood that children will be immunized and, as a result, are associated with lower death rates for infants," notes a 2005 report published by the National Partnership for Women and Families.[10] There is a strong correlation between parental leave entitlements and thriving children—one study found that a year of job-protected *paid* leave is tied to 25 percent fewer post-neonatal deaths, and those benefits continued forward in the child's life with 11 percent fewer deaths of children between one and five years old.[11] Twenty-five percent fewer deaths is a pretty strong argument.

Finally, after more than two weeks in the hospital, Connor was strong enough to go home. Selena delighted in taking her planned time off—partly using accrued paid sick and vacation time, and partly with unpaid leave. Then, like more than half of all mothers of children under one-year-old,[12] and 72 percent of all American mothers, Selena went to work.[13]

Double Whammy

Alfreda, thirty-one, is one of many women facing the overlapping problems of unpaid maternity leave and insufficient childcare options. She loves waking up and walking across her bedroom to see her new son, M'Kai, greet each morning from his crib, "My favorite thing to do with him is to look into his eyes and talk to him because he's a special baby. I really love when he gets up in the morning—he tries to see what's new, adjusts to the lighting, and then he starts laughing. He laughs and he smiles really, really hard and gets cheeky—and I think that's really cute. I've determined he's a morning person. He really likes the morning."

After a lot of soul searching, Alfreda decided to stay home with her second son for the first several months of his life. Using the *unpaid* federal Family and Medical Leave Act, she took a leave of absence from her job of the last seven years, and, as her workplace policy allowed, took 240 hours of advance sick leave (essentially six weeks), which leaves Alfreda with a paid leave deficit that will take two years to earn back. This also left Alfreda without any paid sick or vacation leave for those two years, and in a bind if she or either of her two sons gets sick.

Alfreda found that at six weeks she wasn't ready to go back to work and leave her infant son in the care of others. She decided to stay home and care for him for his early months. In order to do so she had to make the difficult choice between going on welfare and taking out a loan. As of now, she's planning to take out a loan against her future paychecks and is trimming her budget down to the raw edge of comfort, "I'm cutting back on groceries like bread, eggs, milk, and dairy. Things that cost a lot of money—things that are basically essential."

"I'm also giving up 'luxury' driving or frivolous driving. I know I now have to go straight to my son's school, pick him up and bring him back home," says Alfreda. "If I'm visiting a friend in the area, then I'll ask if I can hang out there until I have to pick up my son," just so she doesn't spend the extra gas money.

She's committed to being a good mother and also to nursing her baby. She says the best thing about "being home with my baby is that I get to bond with him and nurse him. If it wasn't for me bonding with the baby, seeing his growth, and the different things that interest him, I'd be back at work because realistically I have to go back."

Her son, M'Kai, nurses ten to twelve times a day, and, unlike her older son who took a bottle easily, absolutely refuses a bottle. "The first time I tried to bottle feed him; he stuck his tongue out to block it. Then every time I tried to put the bottle in he'd move his tongue to stop the bottle. That's how I knew I'd have trouble."

Breastfeeding and paid family leave are tied together.[14] It can be quite hard, sometimes bordering on impossible, to regularly provide an infant with breast milk when the mother has to work full-time immediately after delivery. A Harvard report noted this fact, stating, "Research evidence has shown that paid maternal and paternal leave improves children's health outcomes by making more time available to parents to provide essential care for their children. Paid maternal leave facilitates breastfeeding and reduces the risk of infections. . . . Countries with paid parental leave policies have lower infant mortality and morbidity rates. Paid leave policies also encourage the formation of bonds between parents and children, contributing positively to children's psychosocial development."[15] In fact, in terms of infant mortality rates, the U.S. tied for thirty-eighth in the world with Estonia, Poland, Slovakia, and the United Arab Emirates in 2003.[16]

Alfreda's also worried about putting her infant son in childcare, particularly when he rejects the bottle so vigorously. She's having a difficult time finding an affordable place for him to stay when she goes back to work, although she's been on several waiting lists for infant childcare centers since she got pregnant. And she's concerned about how her son will be treated, "There are a lot of people who watch babies whose nerves are bad, and my baby has a piercing cry. So I worry that they will either just let him cry or not be nice. It just really scares me."

The lack of accessible, affordable, quality infant childcare compounds the problems parents face without paid family leave. Many parents simply have to go back to work to keep their families financially solvent, yet early infant care is often difficult to find and is far more expensive than childcare for older children. In fact, a recent study found a widespread scarcity of infant-toddler childcare in all communities, but particularly in low-income communities, across the nation, and noted that "although finding good-quality infant-toddler childcare can be a critical influence on the well-being of infants and toddlers, finding good-quality infant-toddler childcare can be especially challenging for low-income families."[17]

Without access to infant childcare centers (where, again, she's been on waiting lists since she got pregnant), and without other options, Alfreda's thinking of leaving her infant son with a friend of her sister's when she goes back to work, "There's this one lady that my sister knows. She's kind of moody, but she's really good with kids and I might have to use her. But I really don't want to." Yet Alfreda can't live on loans for too long, and she has no choice but to go back to work while her son is still an infant.

Too many American parents must quickly return to work after the birth of a child. Without viable alternatives, parents frequently end up using low quality infant childcare in order to put food on the table. Often these parents worry about their baby's safety and development. This concern is well-founded as studies show young children have a higher rate of cognitive development in the usually more expensive and inaccessible childcare centers than with less expensive informal in-home care.[18] The outcome of this early lack of support may be felt by this child as she/he goes through school and on into the future.

The First (and Only) State with Paid Family Leave

Christine, a California resident and the sole wage earner in her household, is having a less stressful experience with new parenthood.

At 7:59 A.M. on May 15, 2004, a newborn cry of life pierced a hospital room in San Francisco, California, and Christine became a mother at thirty-three years old: "I was pretty stunned how quickly it all happened."

Just the day before, Christine had closed the office-building door behind her as she left work at 5 P.M. She thought she had at least three weeks until her baby arrived.

She met her husband for an early evening beach walk along a stone path looking down to a sandy shore—a regular walk for them. The only difference she noticed was that she felt more tired than usual, barely making it two hundred yards down the path before turning back.

They left the beach for an Italian restaurant and Christine remembers relishing the pasta as only someone who's eaten for two can understand.

Sometime in the middle of the night her water broke. It was a trickle more than a flood, so Christine waited to call her doctor until the morning. After making an 11 A.M. appointment, she called in sick to work. Her husband picked up "the bag," an accessory Christine thought unnecessary, since her due date was more than three weeks away.

She was wrong. "The doctor took one look at me and sent me right across the street to have a baby," recalls Christine. The doctor's office was next to a big red brick hospital, the same one in which Christine was born. And after getting settled into her cozy peach-colored hospital room, complete with comfy chairs and big picture window, Liam was born without complications.

But Christina's journey into motherhood hadn't started with as few complications as her son's delivery. At one point she found herself thirty-two, pregnant, with a husband who had just been laid off. There were points of sheer panic along the way.

Several months earlier, newly wearing maternity clothes, Christine had pushed up from her desk in northern California and taken a short walk down a corridor of cubicles. She'd requested a meeting with the Human Resources Director at her work, and now it was time to sit down face to face.

Fortunately, the Human Resources Director was among the few with an office door that actually closed in the 150-plus company. It could be a private conversation.

"I reached the physical and emotional point where I needed to face the reality of a new baby and get some answers," says Christine, noting she was starting to feel pretty big and unwieldy. The pressure was on because Christine was the sole wage earner, and, as such, her job provided health insurance and other benefits for the entire family.

In a small neutral-colored office, amidst piles of stacked papers and a general feeling of corporate sterility, Christine's options were laid out with graphs and charts. First, she found out her company, like many others, didn't even have a maternity policy. In fact, very few companies do have family leave policies. "A survey of personnel managers, conducted in 2000, found that just 12 percent of companies offered paid maternity leave and just seven percent offered paid paternity leave," notes a National Partnership for Women and Families report. "Eighty-five percent of respondents reported no maternity or paternity leave benefits."[19]

Sharing what she thought after learning her company didn't have a family leave policy and that the federal Family and Medical Leave Act didn't offer monetary support, Christine comments, "I was really naïve and shocked that federal family leave wasn't paid. I feel like everyone is winging it. It feels like every time family leave time comes up, it's the first time the company faces it. It's not like, 'Oh, this is our policy, and these are your options.' "

After processing the bad news—the fact that her company didn't have a maternity policy, and the federal family leave program was unpaid, she felt the good news sink in—she qualified for paid family leave under a new California state law. Christine recalls her feelings at the time, "I was surprised there was so little, and then relieved to hear about the new California paid family leave—since my husband wasn't working, I was pretty much sick with fear about it for months."

PAID FAMILY LEAVE IN CALIFORNIA—HOW WE WON

by Netsy Firestein, Director of the Labor Project for Working Families

Luck, Timing, and Organizing. That's what it took to pass Paid Family Leave in California in 2002; the nation's most comprehensive paid family leave legislation. Most Californians can now get six weeks of paid family leave benefits through a state disability insurance fund, funded by employee contributions. You never know when the time is right for a paid leave or other campaign so persevere with what you believe in.

Our success followed the outlines of any successful campaign. Advocates built awareness and relationships over time, got support from powerful partners, faced opposition from the business community and succeeded through a combination of grassroots organizing, political pressure, legislative maneuvering, media outreach and compromise.

Key ingredients to our success were:

The labor movement
A well-organized coalition
A strong legislator
Good old fashioned organizing.

Several factors made California fertile ground for a paid family leave

California is the only state in America with paid family leave, and is one of only five states (along with New York, New Jersey, Rhode Island, and Hawaii) with short-term disability payments that can be used for disability due to pregnancy and childbirth. Both programs in California are paid by employee contributions into a state fund. California's Paid Family Leave program began July 1, 2004, and employee costs are minimal. For instance, a campaign. We had an existing infrastructure of other laws and benefits related to paid leave issues; a committed core of advocates with varied areas of expertise; a diverse Coalition of unions and community organizations; the California Labor Federation (state AFL-CIO) which prioritized the issue; research on the low cost of providing a paid family leave benefit; and funding for staff and resources for the campaign.

Though the bill got enormous opposition from the business community, we were able to frame the issue in the press as "caring for families." The Coalition along with the Labor Federation mobilized thousands of union members and community advocates to send postcards and emails, call legislators, get press coverage and generate public support for paid leave. Other organizations jumped in to offer expertise, from press outreach to web based emails.

As it gained momentum, we were able to get more press because it was the first paid family leave legislation in the country and it resonated with the public as "good for families." When the bill got to the Governor's desk, it was an election year and labor drove home the national significance of the decision facing the Governor. We flooded his office will emails, letters and calls from the community as well as from celebrities, national political figures and national labor leaders. The Governor signed the bill on September 23, 2002, a historic day for working families.

—Adapted from "Putting Families First: How California Won the Fight for Paid Family Leave," www.laborproject.org under publications.

low-wage worker would pay about $2.25 per month.[20] Christine's son was born with perfect timing to take advantage of the new program.

Between the new California Paid Family Leave program and California short-term physical disability payments, Christine was able to patch together twelve weeks of partial paid leave (six weeks with from the California paid family leave law, and six

---

**BIG TROUBLE FOR
SINGLE PARENTS**

Imagine what the lack of
paid family leave means
for the ten million single
mothers in our nation who
often have less support and
flexibility than those who
are married. The number of
single mothers in America
went from three million in
1970 to ten million in
2003. Single fathers went
from less than a half million
in 1970 to two million in
2003.

---

weeks from California short-term disability payments).

Geographically speaking, Christine was in a good place.

But what if Christine was in one of the other forty-nine states in our nation? She'd be left in the same situation as Selena, having to go right back to work. Or even like Alfreda, using all her paid sick leave, taking out a loan, and then having to go back to work without any banked paid time off. These are not healthy solutions. For example, the repercussions of using all available sick and vacation days can be profound: There won't be any time off left if the new baby in daycare gets sick. What to do then?

Of the fifty states in our nation, only one has the paid family leave program Christine was able to access. There are two main federal laws that relate to women and childbirth, and neither offers paid leave time: The first is the Pregnancy Discrimination Act, which passed in 1978 and made it illegal to discriminate against working women on the basis of pregnancy or childbirth. Prior to the Pregnancy Discrimination Act, women were often pushed to leave their jobs when they became pregnant or had a baby. The second main federal law is the Family and Medical Leave Act (FMLA), which passed in 1993, and grants a female or male employee working at a large company (fifty or more workers) up to twelve weeks of *unpaid* leave during any twelve-month period for the following reasons: the birth and care of the newborn child of the employee; placement with the employee of a son or daughter for adoption or foster care; caring for an immediate family member (spouse, child, or parent) with a serious health condition; or taking medical leave when the employee is unable to work because of a serious health condition.

Yet the FMLA doesn't cover anyone working at a smaller company (less than fifty workers), leaving a huge portion of our population without any federal coverage at all. A mere 46.5 percent of private-sector employees are both covered by and eligible for FMLA due to the eligibility restrictions that limit it to employees of large companies that have worked there at least 1,250 hours per year for at least twelve months.[21]

For those that do qualify for FMLA, during the unpaid leave the parent retains health benefits and his or her job is guaranteed, but the FMLA doesn't include provisions for paid leave while parents take time out of the workforce. This leaves millions of parents in a financial bind and ultimately unable to take the uncompensated leave the law allows.

The ability for parents to take leave without fear of losing their job is important. That said, "Paid leave significantly decreases infant mortality, while other leave has no significant effect. This suggests that if leave is provided without adequate payment and job protection, parental leave-taking behavior may

WINNING FAMILY CARE LEAVE IN WISCONSIN

by Ellen Bravo, author and former director of 9to5, National Association of
Working Women

Mothers aren't the only ones who care for family members—and newborns aren't the only ones needing care. Wisconsin was one of many states where 9to5 helped build broad coalitions to win a new minimum standard of family and medical leave. In February 1988, after Governor Tommy Thompson announced he'd support only 30 days of maternity leave, our coalition escorted a dozen kids to the Capitol. They told their stories to Secretary of Employment Relations, John Tries.

Noah Michaelson was big for a nine-year-old. It was hard to picture him hairless and skinny from cancer four years earlier. The Racine boy recounted how both his parents would accompany him to treatment, one to hold him and one to tell a story while the needle went in. "Operations and tests hurt more when your parents aren't there," he said. Noah remembered other children at the hospital who were all alone— he understood now that their parents had to be at work or they'd lose their jobs and their insurance.

Chris Chrisler from DeForest was adopted for the first time at the age of twelve. "I was so happy to finally have a home," he'd written. Problem was, Chris and his new brothers and sisters had to go to bed by 8:00 P.M. The adoption agency required their mother to be home during the day, but her employer wouldn't give her leave.

Other children told about losing a grandparent, dealing with a

not be very responsive. . . . As a result, other leave does not have a significant effect on improving infant health," notes an *Economic Journal* report.[22] In other words, it's *paid* family leave that makes the big difference.

sibling with a developmental disability, struggling with asthma. The last and youngest was my son, Craig Miller, then age seven, who'd once been hit by a car. He had a message for the Governor: "How would you like it if your son was sick and you couldn't take time off to be with your sick kid?"

"You know," Tries told them, "we're so used to dealing with lobbyists, we forget about those who are affected by our legislation." He thanked the kids and asked if any of them had a question. Craig immediately raised his hand.

"I want to know why wouldn't the Governor sign this bill?" Tries laughed and promised the Governor would sign some version of family leave.

The kids then held a press conference for legislators and told their stories again—this time adding the Secretary's promise. Newspaper headlines the next day read, "Young 'Lobbyists' Win Lawmakers' Hearts."

A few weeks later, the Governor did sign the Wisconsin Family and Medical Leave Act. It was only the second state law to include time for family care, and the first to allow the right for workers to substitute any accrued paid time for the unpaid leave. Later business lobbyists challenged that provision, claiming men were taking time to go fishing and alligator hunting. Oh, no, we said—finally more men can be good fathers, because they're not being punished for it at work.

—This piece is adapted from her forthcoming book, *Taking on the Big Boys: Reflections from the Feminist Trenches.*

Paid Leave or Bust

Selena, Alfreda, and Christine's experiences give texture to the need for national paid family leave. Although the current law helps many, the twelve weeks of *unpaid* leave is not available to all employees and ignores the very real financial strains most families endure when they are having children. For those with better financial means, the current law allows some comfort that their job will be there after they take some time off to have children. Many families also need the option of taking far more time off than the twelve weeks guaranteed under current law. The current act is a start, not an ending.

Some states are slowly moving forward to increase the help they give new families. A report, *Expecting Better: A State-By-State Analysis of Parental Leave Programs,* uses ten legislative indicators to rate the types of assistance states give:[23]

- Family Leave Benefits
- Medical/Maternity Leave Benefits
- Flexible Sick Days
- At-Home Infant Care Benefits
- Expanded Job-Protected Family Leave
- Expanded Job-Protected Medical/Maternity Leave
- Extended Length of Job-Protected Family and Medical Leave
- State Family Medical Leave Laws
- Paid Family and Medical Leave Benefits for State Employees
- Extended Length of Job-Protected Family and Medical Leave for State Employees

Most of the state columns are woefully blank in the report. In fact, a full nineteen states don't have any of the above legislation.

Bright spots are showing up across the nation, however, with several states making progress. "There are a lot of different states that are chipping away at the issue—some states have laws where you can use your sick time to take care of your child or family member; some states have lowered the eligibility for using the FMLA to twenty-five employees; and some states are trying to improve on FMLA in other ways," points out Netsy Firestein, Director of the Labor Project for Working Families. Given those successes, what's ultimately needed is still a national *paid* family leave law.

YOUNG FAMILIES IN TROUBLE

Most mothers and fathers are in their mid-twenties when their babies are born. This younger age group is still launching their careers, just beginning see their earning potentials rise, and is much less likely to be able to bridge the gap of even a few weeks without a parent's income.

Some companies and organizations are individually trying to find ways to support new parents in the workplace. Selena's non-profit workplace is one such place. After Selena's time home with her premature son was up, she went straight back to work—and she took her newborn son with her.

In an office of fifteen people positioned in cubicles throughout two large rooms that were joined by an enclosed conference room in the center, Selena had a space in the back corner complete with a window and two desks. The utilitarian grey blue décor—desk, cubical walls, carpet—was quickly transformed when a fuzzy cream colored blanket for tummy time was laid over the staid carpeting, an electronic bouncy chair was moved in next to Selena's desk, and a cozy reclining infant car seat was placed next to the hallway. Her second desk became a changing table. A happy, gurgling baby completed the transformation.

Selena had been in her job for three years when she had Connor. She needed to work in order to bring home money to help keep her family afloat, but she also wanted time with her new baby. "I wanted some time for us to bond, especially since we got such a rocky start." The studies that report putting newborns in childcare isn't good for them worried her. Like many new parents, Selena had deeper emotional issues at play as well, "It scared and worried me just to think of leaving him before he was three months old. It made me sad because I didn't want to give him away, I just got him. I worked very hard for him, and I wanted to have him with me all the time."

Selena had never been comfortable with the idea of putting her new baby in childcare before he was three months old. Fortunately he could then go to the same trusted childcare provider that watched his older brother. Once he was born her mind was made up. She wanted Connor with her at work.

She recalls, "I asked if bringing Connor to work would be an option before he was born." Her employer said they could discuss the option after he was born. Then when Connor was born, "I convinced the Executive Director that he had the perfect temperament for this arrangement. I desperately wanted to be with him and was very grateful to be able to spend time with him while earning the money I needed to feed and diaper him," says Selena.

Her co-workers and supervisor were incredibly helpful. She comments, "It's an office of all women who love babies." Every afternoon one of her co-workers would take Connor for a walk around the building, usually at about 2 P.M. Another co-worker was in charge of taking care of him every time Selena had to go to a meeting, and still another co-worker took him for about a half hour every day to play. It was a team effort.

For her part, Selena perfected the art of using a half moon-shaped blue Boppy pillow to hold her baby so she could breast-feed and type on her computer keyboard at the same time. At three months old, Connor started going to the childcare provider during the day as planned, and Selena remains employed at the same place now two years later.

This is a heartening example of an organization that found a way for a new parent to work with an infant. Since the United States doesn't have a structure to support new parents in our society, Selena's family likely would have been one of the families reflected in the statistic that 25 percent of new "poverty spells" start when a baby is born. Since her workplace stepped up to the plate, Selena did not have to face the excruciating choice of leaving her tiny baby or facing a "poverty spell."[24]

Unfortunately, not that many employers can or will offer that kind of flexibility to new parents. Selena's solution isn't widely available or possible in all jobs. There's still a clear need for a national paid family leave program—not just for parents, but for businesses as well.

There are very real negative impacts on businesses due to the lack of a paid family leave policy in the United States. In *The Price of Motherhood,* Ann Crittenden writes, "With no right to a paid leave, many American mothers who want to stay at home with a new baby simply quit their jobs, and this interruption in employment costs them dearly in terms of lost income." This turnover in employees cost companies too. Paid family leave is shown to also benefit employers by saving them the costs of recruitment and training due to high employee turnover, and leading to greater job satisfaction which then translates to higher worker productivity.[25]

In each of the stories shared—that of Selena, Alfreda, and Christine—the edges of other motherhood issues are waiting to take center stage. The need for paid family leave comes at the beginning of a family life that commences with the birth of a daughter or son. As babies grow older, parents need work that allows them to also fulfill their family responsibilities. Flexible work hours, affordable healthcare, quality childcare, and living wages are critical pieces that, along with paid family leave, are all needed in order to help our families flourish. To truly value and support our nations' children we must provide a solid foundation. Providing paid family leave is the first step.

Currently mothers are punished simply for being mothers— they are forced to make choices no one should have to make by mortgaging their futures to take care of their babies. Babies require a period of intensive love and attention from their caregivers. Parents should be able to choose to provide this care joyfully, not under the threat of financial ruin. These babies are our most basic natural resource. In thirty years, when today's adults are getting older, these babies will be the economic engine of our nation. We need to be sure our children have been provided with the nurturance required to become strong, intelligent citizens that carry our nation into the future.

Paid family leave is not a lofty idea, but rather a basic structural support we must put in place to ensure the health of our children and to make motherhood compatible with the workplace. We call on the nation, and every state within it, to give American mothers and families this critical support.

Manifesto Point "M"

Mothers need time to have babies. Giving a mother no choice but to come back to work mere days after the birth of a child or face financial ruin is bad social policy. Society needs to share the cost of bringing new life into the world.

ACTION: Mothers want

(1) Paid family leave for parents with a new child in the home.

(2) Short-term disability leave for childbirth recovery comparable in scope to other developed nations.

International Paid Family Leave Comparisons

•   **The United States does not offer paid family leave.** In fact, the United States is the only industrialized country in the world that doesn't have *paid* leave other than Australia (which does give a full year of guaranteed unpaid leave to all women, compared with the only 12 weeks of unpaid leave given to those who work for companies with more than fifty employees in the U.S.).[i] There is one state in America, California, which implemented a six-week paid family program in July of 2004 for California residents.

•   **A full 163 countries give women paid leave with the birth of a child.**[ii] Forty-five countries give fathers a right to paid parental leave as well.[iii]

•   **Canada gives birth mothers fifteen weeks of partial paid leave for physical recovery, and then also gives another thirty-five weeks of partial paid parental leave that has to be taken before the child turns one-year-old.** This thirty-five weeks of parental leave can be taken by the mother or the father, or can be shared between the two. The pay during the *fifty weeks total of leave* related to a new child is 55 percent of the average gross salary over the past twenty-six calendar weeks.[iv] All in all, there are fifty weeks of partially paid leave available for new Canadian parents to spend with their child.

•   **Sweden, with about a year of paid family leave and some time specifically reserved for fathers, is often used as a model of exemplary family leave policy for other nations.**[v] According to the European Industrial Relations Observatory (EIRO), in Sweden, "Parental leave runs for 480 days, of which 390 days are paid at the same rate as for sick pay—i.e. 80 percent of normal pay (up to a ceiling). Parents each have a legal right to take 50 percent of the leave, but one parent can transfer some of their entitlement to the other. However, 60 days of the leave may not be transferred. This part of the leave is called the 'mother months' and 'father months' respectively."[vi] Sweden not only offers a very long paid leave, but that leave is significant because some is reserved for fathers as a way to establish better equality between men and women. By many accounts, this model is working. "Wives earn 39 percent of after-tax family income, the highest percentage in the world,"[vii] writes Ann Crittenden in *The Price of Motherhood* of Sweden. In addition, a positive correlation has been found between those fathers that care for their babies and long term involvement with those children.

i. http://www.hsph.harvard.edu/globalworkingfamilies/images/report.pdf

ii. http://www.hsph.harvard.edu/globalworkingfamilies/images/report.pdf

iii. http://www.hsph.harvard.edu/globalworkingfamilies/images/report.pdf

iv http://www.hrsdc.gc.ca/asp/gateway.asp?hr=en/ei/types/special.shtml&hs=tyt#Maternity3

v. http://www.eiro.eurofound.eu.int/2004/06/inbrief/se0406102n.html

vi. Ann Crittenden, The Price of Motherhood, pages 239–250. Quote p. 248

To take action go to **www.MotherhoodManifesto.com**.

3

Open Flexible Work

Outdoor speakers blared Top 40 hits ranging from U2's "Vertigo" to Hilary Duff's sugary pop grooves as school children walked laps, laps, and more laps around a ribbon-marked field. With music in the air, the sun shining down on her shoulders, and purple pen in hand, Dr. Jennifer Stone bounced to the beat while leaning over to check off laps on children's jerseys as they successfully completed another round. It was the annual walk-a-thon to raise money for the elementary school and Dr. Stone was volunteering.

This is the same Dr. Stone who enters a four-story brick building through double white doors each and every weekday morning, who thrives in an environment of calm efficiency. Dr. Stone, volunteer and mom, also has a Ph.D. in neuroanatomy, and works as a researcher and professor in the field of otolaryngology (ear, nose, and throat medicine) at the University of Washington.

Her office, neatly lined with books and scientific journals from nearly floor to ceiling, serves as a work base. An overcrowded desk is tucked into a corner topped with a computer as well as pictures of her daughters and husband, which provide bright spots in the organized chaos of academia.

During the day, Dr. Stone moves effortlessly from hi-tech digital compound microscope, to autoclave, to sectioning stations where developing chicken ears are sliced paper thin, to viral injection stations where genetic modifications on chicken embryos begin. She studies how chickens regenerate the tiny hair cells in the inner ear that are integral to hearing. Dr. Stone is searching for a way to replicate that regeneration in humans who, once those particular cells are damaged, lose hearing permanently.

Dr. Stone is a mother of two, Rebecca, age five, and Olivia, age six.

While regularly working more than 40 hours per week, Dr. Stone can also be found at school performances, baseball practice, the annual field day, jump rope shows, and, of course, walk-a-thons. An active, engaged mother, Dr. Stone engineered a flex-time job structure that works for her and her family.

"I basically work from 9:30 A.M. until 4:30 P.M. and then at least two hours again at night after the kids go to bed," she explains. When she takes time out during the day for school or other family activities, Dr. Stone makes up that time before or after her regular lab and office hours—often in the dark, early mornings or late, late nights. In the end, "Like most in the sciences, I work a lot more than 40 hours per week. There's a lot of pressure to be on top of the literature, to be writing and publishing journal articles about research, so there's no way I could be part-time, though I do have the flexibility to work anytime I want."

> **FLEXTIME MISCONCEPTIONS**
>
> The primary myth surrounding flextime is that it always means part-time or reduced hour jobs. Not so. One of the most important types of flextime is flexibility in the time worked during the day. In fact, that very type of flextime was listed as one of the top ways for companies to "accommodate the nonlinear realities of women's work lives" in an extensive March 2005 Harvard Business Review research report.[50]

A survey of working women reported in the Harvard Business Review confirms that Dr. Stone isn't the only mom placing work flexibility as a high priority: the majority of women surveyed (64 percent) reported flexible work arrangements as "either extremely or very important to them." The survey also found that "by a considerable margin, highly qualified women find flexibility more important than compensation; only 42 percent say that 'earning a lot of money' is an important motivator."[1]

Highly qualified and generally fairly well paid women are the most likely to find or demand flexible schedules. Women with low income jobs also need flexibility, yet are the least likely to

BETTER SOLUTIONS FOR ALL

A survey of highly qualified working women for a *Harvard Business Review* study found that 43 percent of highly qualified working women who have children took time out of the workforce to care for family members. Of these women, 93 percent want to return to their careers. Not only do women take a wage hit for leaving the workplace, businesses end up taking big monetary hits in retraining and hiring costs. Both businesses and families benefit when policies that allow parents to successfully juggle work and family are in place.[51]

have flexible work options—these are also the very moms who are more likely to struggle with access to affordable childcare, and who are least likely to have paid family or other leave.[2]

Low income jobs are often rigidly confined by the clock. One single mother of two children under five-years-old had a horrible experience with an inflexible schedule.[3] She worked the night shift at a psychiatric center in upstate New York and had a sitter watch her children at night. Her supervisor requested that she work mandatory overtime with a fair degree of regularity, and she frequently was only given a couple of hours notice. She simply couldn't do it.

To make a long story short: She couldn't work the overtime because her sitter also had a day job. After saying no twice and getting cited for misconduct (even though she said she could work a partial shift or bring her children in to sleep at work), she was fired. Her union took up the cause and got her job back. The arbitrator commented, "No person should be forced to choose between his children or his livelihood"[4] and worked out a deal where she was fined $1.00 for technical insubordination, retained her job, and ordered her to give her employer thirty days notice of three days each month that she would work an overtime shift. This small increase of flexibility in scheduling made the critical difference that allowed her to keep the job that supported her two growing children. It also gave her employer three dependable overtime shifts each month.[5]

From the highly paid to those making minimum wage, far too few women in America have flexible work options—almost three-fourths of working adults state they don't control their work schedules.[6] In fact, the top reason noted by highly educated and trained women for leaving the "fast track" is the lack of family time.[7] The lack of flexible work options often leads women to quit needed jobs.

This is a problem because most families need two working parents to support their family, many women want and need to continue their careers, and when women take time out of the workforce they face huge wage hits, or pay cuts, when they later return (as 74 percent do within two years). These wage hits take a life-long toll: On average, women take an 18 percent cut in their pay, a significant wage hit, for an average of 2.2 years out of the labor force—with women in business sectors taking an increased hit of 28 percent. For those women who stay out of the labor force for three or more years, the news is even bleaker: A 37 percent loss of earning power.[8]

Even after women come back into the workforce, the wage hits, which do get smaller over time, still persist for decades.[9] This is a tremendous economic burden, which not only impacts

THE MYTH OF THE "IDEAL" WORKER

Most employers organize work "around the ideal worker who works full-time and takes little or no time off for childbearing or childrearing," writes Joan Williams in her groundbreaking book *Unbending Gender: Why Family and Work Conflict and What to Do About It.* This "ideal worker" is expected to work 60 hours per week without questions, be available on short notice, and travel as needed. The "ideal" worker expectation is unrealistic for many working parents who have parental responsibilities.

women's ability to support their family, but also impacts future retirement because of lost income, and as Ann Crittenden writes, "a college-educated woman with one child can easily pay a "Mommy tax' (lost lifetime earnings) of $1 million."

Widespread implementation of workplace flextime policies will go a long way towards helping women maintain viable careers and remain economically stable while having families. Businesses also benefit with higher employee retention, lower training and recruiting costs, and better employee performance.[10]

With a looming labor crunch[11] many businesses are also looking for ways to retain employees. With this in mind, the Harvard report details some solutions for businesses to keep talented women in the workforce: "Reduced-hour jobs, flexible work-days, and removal of off-ramping's stigma are just a few strategies."[12]

Detect a theme here? Flexibility.

Work flexibility is sometimes difficult to quickly explain because it is, in and of itself, flexible. Flexible work options can vary depending on employer and employee needs. Some options include having a set number of weekly hours that can be worked whenever the employee schedules the time; part-time work; compressed work weeks; telecommuting or working from home; being able to choose work shifts; and more. Studies show flextime allows for a more balanced life and productive workplace.[13]

Like many parents, Dr. Stone finds that flextime actually makes her better at her job by allowing her to more successfully juggle work and family. "Kids have given me the best incentive to be on top of my busy schedule. I do a lot more planning and manage my calendar more aggressively. Without this increased organization I wouldn't have quality time with my family, so in a sense the family has motivated the organization, and the benefits from that organization have fed into my work."

The notion of the "ideal" worker, who can be at the office from 9 A.M.–6 P.M. or 9 A.M.–7 P.M. (or later) every day of the week and can travel at a moment's notice, simply doesn't take into account the needs of contemporary mothers, families, and children. It's not always a question of working fewer hours, but it is also a question of working smarter hours that are conducive to the demands of career, family, and business. Rather than forcing mothers to conform to schedules that are often incompatible with the demands of child rearing, flexible work options allow parents to create work schedules that are well suited to raising happy, healthy children.

Companies Taking the Lead

For all practical purposes, the Johnson Moving and Storage office, located just outside of Denver, Colorado, looks just like any typical American office. Florescent ceiling lights illuminate rows of cubicles, and the muted sounds of people working fill the air. But the real center of this particular office, one of nine Johnson Moving and Storage offices in nine cities that span six states, can be found by walking down an 80-foot corridor lined with often-empty cubicles. At the end of this long hall is a doorway.

The door opens to a small room abuzz with the hum of small fans cooling racks of computers and high powered servers. The darkness is broken by the blinking of LEDs. This temperature-controlled room is a hub for the 107-year-old company, housing the main phone system that can be accessed via the internet from any location, all of the digitized files (and all files are digitized), and any other information an employee would need to work anytime from anywhere.

And they do mean anywhere. One off-site bookkeeping employee works in Pakistan. He moved because his wife missed

---

DEFINITION OF FLEXIBILITY

from "The Families and Work Institute",
http://familiesandwork.org/3w/about/definition.html

Flexibility is a way to define how and when work gets done and how careers are organized. Workplace flexibility may include:

- Having traditional flextime (setting daily hours within a range periodically)
- Having daily flextime
- Being allowed to take time off during the work day to address family matters
- Being able to take a few days off to care for a sick child without losing pay, having to use vacation days, or make up an excuse for absence
- Being able to work some regular hours at home

her home country, but kept his job. In fact, this particular employee now enjoys the added bonus of being in a different time zone, so he can work through our night/his day to meet deadlines. In fact, a full 25 percent of all the nearly 100 Johnson Moving and Storage employees, including contract workers, are off-site or virtual workers (17.1 percent of in-house staff work off-site). Many also work flexible hours to fit their family or personal schedules.

Owner Jim Johnson, a self-described conservative, made the leap to cutting-edge workplace policies in the late nineties after hearing Joan Williams, author of *Unbending Gender*, speak at a Harvard Divinity Club function held in the parlor of a private turn-of-the-century home in Denver. "My wife saw Joan Williams' presentation in the morning and she wanted me to go in the afternoon. We have twin girls, and my wife's an attorney.

- Being able to take breaks when one wants to
- Having a work shift that is desirable
- Having complete or a lot of control over work schedule
- Being able to work part-time (if currently full-time) or full-time (if currently part-time) in one's current position
- Being able to work a compressed work week
- Being able to work part-year in current position
- Seldom being required to work paid or unpaid overtime with little or no notice
- Believing that one can use flexible work arrangements without jeopardizing job advancement

The 2002 National Study of the Changing Workforce, Families and Work Institute used an index of the flexible workplace based upon the thirteen specific measures listed above.

At the time she was really struggling with being an excellent attorney and an excellent parent." Johnson went to the presentation and was changed.

"One of the things that struck me with Joan Williams' presentation was that the order of traditional society—which was God, family, then work—had been flipped in later industrial cultures and it just didn't work. It struck me as being a truthful statement," recalls Johnson. He comments that, "A lot of these issues are infused with political overtones and it was so refreshing to have it told in a rational way. It made a lot of sense to recreate the workplace in a better way."

Johnson was also drawn in by the business possibilities in what then was a very tight employment market. So he decided to give it a try.

He first spoke with the vice president in charge of administrative staff, and asked her what she thought of offering some of the employees the option to work either fully or part-time at home. She was excited, and after talking with other staff, she returned to tell Johnson the response was overwhelmingly positive.

Johnson Moving and Storage executives then got to work defining individual jobs according to goals rather than just by hours worked and the location where the job was done. This approach is being used with increasing frequency. A July 2005 *Time* magazine article highlights this trend by focusing on the recent changes made at Best Buy, which is shifting its business culture to a results-oriented work environment (ROWE) in much the same way as Johnson Moving and Storage.[14]

After experimenting with ROWE, Best Buy had interesting early results. The *Time* magazine article reports that Best Buy analyzed a fairly small sample of three hundred employees and found that after implementing ROWE, "Turnover in the first three months of employment fell from 14 percent to zero, job satisfaction rose 10 percent, and their team performance scores rose 13 percent." There is a slow transition at Best Buy to this new working model. Different teams opt into the ROWE program as it makes sense for them.

One important factor is that the Best Buy employees opt in as teams, so there isn't prejudice against individual employees using the new working model.[15] This is important to note because many employees using flextime report hostility from other non-flextime employees. This hostility can hamper the career path of people using flexible work options. In fact, a study in the *Harvard Business Report* notes, "Of flexible work arrangements in general, 21 percent report that 'there is an unspoken rule at my workplace that people who use those options will not be promoted.' "[16] The fact that Best Buy is getting rid of the stigma of flexible work options may be one of the reasons their shift to the new working model is successful. It's going so well that in the Minneapolis Best Buy headquarters, about half of the 3,500 employees are now part of the program, with the percentage expected to increase over time.[17]

Johnson explains how they made the shift in his moving and storage company, "We detached what needed to be done from the hours needed to do it. We weren't trying to get 60 hours of work for 40 hours of pay, but we said as long as we don't get any complaints [from customers] we really don't care when you do your work; and as long as you respond in an appropriate manner, we don't care what part of your day is available."

This policy necessarily applied to jobs that were fairly independent from the constructs of time and space—primarily accounting and administrative functions where immediate answers weren't needed, and a home office environment was often more productive than a cubicle (and a cost-saving measure for the company in terms of overhead). Other employees couldn't take advantage of this type of flextime policy because they need to be available at distinct times. For example, the movers and staff that coordinate between the dispatch crew and customers need to be available during set hours in order for the business to operate efficiently. Even some move coordinators, however, work at home during set hours.

The policy changes brought glowing reports from employees, some writing to Johnson to tell him about their experience:

—"For me, in my over 19 years at Johnson's, this work-at-home phase has been the most rewarding."

—"Working from home allows me to arrange my work hours with a twenty-four-hour window, rather than an eight-hour window. This work set-up allows me to be a mom first, still accomplish my responsibilities to my employer, and pull in a paycheck."

—One single father notes that he saves the cost of gas from commuting to work, and comments, "I can take my daughter to school and pick her up.... The option to work at home is truly appreciated."

—"If my kids are sick I can be at home and still work," comments one mother. She also adds, "Thank you for giving me the ability to be a good mom and wife, and still have a career."

—"I can concentrate on tasks I'm doing. There aren't any more interruptions from other employees in regards to personal problems or other work related problems."

—"I'm able to complete my tasks and feel more productive."

—"In 2003, my husband suffered a fall and broke his ankle. I was able to be home and close to him."

—"The money I saved in daycare alone was hundreds of dollars per month. I was seriously injured this year, and in a wheelchair for five months. Had I not been able to work from home, I wouldn't have been able to work at all."

The flexible work options weren't just helping the employees; Johnson found that his company also experienced benefits. First, like at Best Buy, the employee turnover dropped significantly, falling to half that of the regular office staff without flextime. "You can see why," Johnson comments, "because as life changes, those occurrences don't prompt a resignation."

Another business benefit is that Johnson can now hire better-qualified people who would otherwise need to be paid more for their positions than he is able to afford. Those people are willing to trade lower salaries for working at home since they don't have added costs related to working outside of the home, such as paying for gas and daycare. "I suspect I'd have more wage pressure from employees without the work-at-home option." He also finds he gets a higher caliber of people applying for positions with flextime options, noting, "That talent would be out of the job market without the work-at-home option."

All in all, Johnson notes, "We're definitely getting higher quality employees because of the work-at-home program. I have a competitive advantage because apparently not many other employers are replicating this type of work, so our general talent pool selection is better."

Studies show that Johnson isn't the only businessperson that has found flextime options can be beneficial to both the employer and employee. A Families and Work Institute report, *The 2005 National Study of Employers*, found that half (47 percent) of the companies that offer work life initiatives including flexible work schedules, family leave, and childcare, do so not because they want to altruistically support employees, but because it makes better business sense given efforts to recruit and retain employees, and many businesses (25 percent) reported they do so to increase the productivity and job commitment of employees.[18]

Quite interestingly, that same study found that small companies, those with fifty to ninety-nine employees, are the most likely to allow workplace flexibility options.[19] Not all flextime options are as loose as the models used by Johnson Moving and

Storage and Best Buy. As previously noted, flexible work options differ according to workplace needs.

Successful budget airline Jet Blue takes a more structured approach to flextime, allowing its airline reservation representatives to work split shifts from home offices.

Susan, a mother of three young boys from eight to thirteen years old, is one such employee. As you walk in the front door of Susan's house, there aren't any clues that the home office behind the closed door in the hallway is actually a satellite to Jet Blue's corporate headquarters. The cozy colonial decor brings warmth to this house of five people. A focal point for family gatherings is the dark cherry dining room table with claw feet and matching high back chairs that were all brought to this Utah town by covered wagon from the east coast three generations ago. This table certainly doesn't look like it belongs in a break area for an airline satellite office, but in this case it does.

Susan takes Jet Blue reservations from her home office, working between fifteen and twenty-four hours each week and choosing her own daily shifts. There are about 1,200 people holding similar jobs for Jet Blue, which handles all reservations via people working from home, and offers a wide variety of set shifts and schedules. Their compensation includes an hourly pay rate that generally starts under ten dollars an hour, profit sharing, and free flight benefits.

These jobs are very popular—many in the Salt Lake City community hear about them by word of mouth. When the company puts out a call for new applicants three or four times each year, they regularly get over 1,000 applicants in the first 48 hours after posting the jobs.

Susan's current schedule is planned around the times her children are in school and the times her husband can be at home watching the kids. "I have a schedule of Tuesdays, Thursdays, and Saturdays. I work from 11 A.M. until 2 P.M. and then from 6 P.M. until 9 P.M. on those same days. So it's a split shift three days a week," she explains.

"I was working outside of home before Jet Blue, and it was very disruptive, getting up early and getting everyone ready and taking them somewhere." She adds that working from home is much better.

Her home office is set up for efficiency. When she was hired, Jet Blue came in and installed a dedicated computer and phone. She starts each shift by turning on her Jet Blue computer and signing into their phone system (she also has her own personal computer in her office). "We have a separate line for home and we have two lines for Jet Blue—one is for calls coming in and the other is for outgoing support calls in case I have questions during reservations."

The reservation calls come in constantly while she's on her shift. The minute she hangs up with one call another one rings in. She handles these calls with ease, and enjoys her exchanges with the customers, "I do have fun talking with people. There are some difficult ones, but for the most part people are nice and happy to be planning a trip.

"Now you know why we're the only airline that's not in

bankruptcy. We treat our customers really well, we're happy to be working for a really great company, and it's great to be able to work at home. It works out really well for all of us: For the company because the customer is happy and the employee is happy," she concludes.

From the business side, Steve Mayne, Jet Blue's operations manager concurs, "As a company we are very, very satisfied and happy with the way this has panned out for us." He continues, and shares the company philosophy, "We feel that if we have very satisfied employees working from home, then that satisfaction will transfer to the customer who will also enjoy doing business with Jet Blue and tell others which will also bring in repeat business." He concludes, "It's absolutely working."

As we move into a Digital Age, those companies that use flexible work options often have more effective workplaces.[20] In fact, the Families and Work Institute includes flexible workplaces as one of the six criteria for creating an effective workplace, and notes that their own research "consistently reveals that flexibility is linked to engagement, retention, job satisfaction, and employee well-being."[21] Increased access to flexible work options can benefit both the employer and employee.

After seeing the benefits of flexible work arrangements, many countries have passed national legislation to make that option more widely available. Great Britain, for example, passed national legislation in 2003 that gives parents of children under the age of six the right to request flexible work. This law sets a process for the request: An employee makes a written request to their employer; a discussion is held between the two, then the employer grants or denies the request. The employee is given an appeal process if they don't agree with the answer. The employer was given several broad grounds to legally deny the flexibility request, including if the arrangement will cost the business money or otherwise hurt their ability to conduct commerce.[22]

As of 2005, this type of legislation hasn't passed in the United States. Shelley Waters Boots, acting director of the Work and Family Program at the New America Foundation, notes that some members of Congress are considering proposing flexible work legislation. Putting this type of legislation forward is an important step to increase public and legislator awareness about the need for, and possibilities of, such legislation.

"Families, and especially parents, really need to stand up and say flexible work options are an important part of being both a good parent and a good worker," notes Waters Boots. "It shouldn't be an either/or decision, as in either time or families. We need to figure out how, as a country, we can allow people to be good at both roles."

Some parents and employees are getting active and requesting flexible work arrangements here in the United States (although flexible work options aren't yet widely available).[23] Judy David Bloomfield, director of One Small Step, points out that right now, "Most flexible work arrangements are negotiated between the employee and the boss. Flexible work arrangements have become more prevalent because there is a groundswell with employees. But it still takes individuals to take the initiative to make these things happen. The flip side is that it takes managers willing to work it out. We've still got a long way to go. There is still a lot of manager resistance. But what I do see is that in companies that are doing these types of things, there is more and more sharing of success stories and those stories are being shared through the company."

By most accounts the biggest workplace impacts come when individuals—employees, managers, or business owners—take the initiative to create flexible work options in their workplaces. Often the flexible-work trailblazer opens up opportunities for co-workers to also make flexible working arrangements as businesses realize this type of work can help their bottom line. An essay written by Carol Ostrom in the book, *Take Back Your Time*,[24] shares how she and two co-workers finally got their management to agree to a flexible job-share arrangement where three people worked two jobs at a major newspaper.

Carol's first few requests for a job share position failed mainly because they were centered on herself and not on the workplace advantages. She writes, "I remember saying—quite eloquently, I imagined at the moment—how much I loved writing, loved journalism, but that other parts of my life were demanding attention, and they were parts I could no longer put 'on hold.'" This wasn't the best argument to management who were more concerned about an efficient workplace than Carol's home pressures, and promptly declined the request.

Carol didn't give up, finally realizing what she describes in her essay as "Lesson Number One: Getting a job share is not about you. It's never about you, no matter what your company says. It's about your company's needs." She writes, "We got our job share, finally, because newsroom managers wanted desperately to hire someone with specific skills for a particular position. The money wasn't in the budget, and managers didn't see any coming down the pike. But the job share, we noted repeatedly, after we finally caught the drift, would be a way to "gain" a position. . . . The point is that it might have gone a lot more smoothly for us if we'd figured out earlier that it wasn't about us."

The job share was successful. The three workers split the two jobs by months (four months working, and then two months off) to allow each of them to work on long-term projects, rather than a more traditional job-share that splits each workweek. And, they did blaze a trail for others in their workplace to also have flexible work arrangements, including one editor who, years earlier, was very hesitant about allowing this type of work arrangement and now holds a part-time job share position herself. Carol writes, "Sometimes we kid her now about her earlier opposition. She knows we understand."

The Part-Time Paridigm

The office windows were open, and a hot summer breeze carried the distant noise of traffic up five stories and into the Environmental Media Services West (now Resource Media) office. It was

the weekly staff meeting that happened every Monday at 10 A.M.
Liz, northwest director of the non-profit communications firm
for environmental and public health issues, had important news
to share with her staff of four—news that had been hard to keep
secret in the close quarters of their workplace.

Their office was set up newsroom style: A big open room with
desks lining the walls, and a sleek, but somewhat faded, conference table situated in the center. An enlarged, framed comic
hangs on one wall. This comic spoke to the work generated from
the room: Two cowboys were sitting around a campfire with an
old fashioned coffee pot warming in the flames. One cowboy said
to the other, "Hank, rustle me up some of that fairly traded,
songbird-friendly organic breakfast blend yer brewin'."

The comic was hung in honor of the songbird-friendly coffee
campaign they'd been working on for the Seattle Audubon
Society. Liz recalls the feeling of, "Ah, now that we've made it
into the comics, we've really made it!" The women who worked
in the office were all widely respected for effectively generating
media for their clients.

Liz had something out of the ordinary to say at this particular
staff meeting. She'd been holding back her news for weeks now.
That something had her plotting out exactly where the bathroom
was in every place she entered, carrying a plastic bag on the
metro bus "just in case," and brought her a new understanding
of just how far the bathroom was from her office door (fifteen
feet straight out and ten feet to the left).

Liz was twelve weeks pregnant, and had been battling morning, noon, and evening sickness for the past month.

"I was so sick, but I didn't want to tell anyone for ten or twelve weeks until I knew the pregnancy was going to 'stick,' and I remember thinking, 'How am I going to hide this?' " recalls Liz. She also remembers feeling an enormous amount of relief when she dropped her bombshell during that Monday morning staff meeting, "By the time I told everyone, I was so relieved that I could finally say why I looked like I just stepped off a seventeen hour plane trip from Singapore every morning. "

During those weeks of waiting to tell her staff, Liz did her homework on the home front. She visited several childcare facilities, had discussions with other mothers about how to really balance work and family (Several recommend that six months was the ideal time off because it gives time to bond with the baby, yet is before separation anxiety starts full force. Many emphasized, "Three months is too short, it's just too short."); and finally chose the childcare center she eventually wanted to use.

This decision caused a cascade of other linked decisions to follow. Signing up for childcare required getting on a waiting list for a start date on a specific month and year. This requirement made it necessary for Liz to think long and hard about what she wanted to do after her baby was born. So by the time she shared her news with co-workers, Liz already had her unborn child on a childcare waiting list, had decided to take six months off, and also was sure she wanted to work part-time when she came back.

"The precedent was already set in our office that new moms were getting their jobs back part-time if they wanted. Precedents are key because the first person to break the precedent has it the hardest, and I wasn't the first," she shares. The precedent was buoyed by the fact that the general situation was tipped in "new moms' favor because it's hard to find replacements for this type of work where established relationships with reporters are highly prized. So allowing people to work part-time is a way to retain the talent," says Liz.

In the back of her mind, Liz knew that after having children she wanted a balanced work schedule that didn't include five or more sunset to sundown days at the office each week. She comments, "Being part-time after Aaron was born was always in the cards." In fact, studies show that Liz was onto something, professionals who work part-time are less likely to report work and family conflicts than those choosing a full-time position.[25] Unfortunately, part-time positions in this country usually come with a pay cut and few, if any, benefits.

Liz, however, had a different experience. When Liz returned from her six months home with the baby to work a part-time schedule of twenty-six hours per week, her hourly wage equivalency stayed the same as when she left at full-time. In stark contrast to Liz's experience, people taking part-time jobs commonly receive lower pay than if they were working a similar job full-time. A 2002 National Study of the Changing Workforce notes this trend, finding that even co-workers notice part-timers get a

---

IT'S NOT JUST MOTHERS

by John de Graaf, National Coordinator of *Take Back Your Time*

Though working mothers may be the most pressed for time and in need of relief, America's time poverty crisis affects nearly everyone. American work hours have been climbing slowly, but steadily since the mid-1970s and today, the average American works nine weeks—350 hours—more each year than the average Western European.

Increased working hours threaten our quality of life in many ways:

Americans increasingly recognize the impacts of time poverty on their lives. According to a November 28, 2005, *Fortune* magazine study, even corporate CEOs now want more time outside work (84 percent), even if it means making less money (55 percent). The same article pointed out that many European countries are actually more productive

---

raw deal: 61 percent of employees who work with a mixture of full- and part-time co-workers say, "part-timers receive less than pro rata pay and benefits compared with full-time employees in the same positions just because they work part-time."[26]

Liz is also faring well in another area that is a common pitfall with part-time positions: She has full medical and dental coverage in her part-time position (the same as when she was working full-time). This full coverage is quite unusual. The vast majority of part-time workers don't have any healthcare coverage (81 percent).[27] Most other benefits that full-time workers receive—such as vacation leave, sick leave, pensions, and life insurance—are also often absent, even in a pro-rated manner, from part-time work packages.[28]

In fact, the rising cost of healthcare is one of the big hurdles to

per worker hour than the U.S. is. And a recent report of the World Economic Forum found that several of the world's most competitive economies are in Scandinavia, where shorter work hours and generous paid leave policies are taken for granted.

Europeans enjoy multiple legal protections of their right to time, including four weeks of paid vacation after a year on the job, paid sick leave, limits on the length of their work weeks, generous paid family leave benefits (which also apply to fathers), and increasingly, the right to choose part-time work, while retaining the same hourly pay, healthcare, opportunities for promotions and other, pro-rated, benefits.

A new campaign, TAKE BACK YOUR TIME (www.timeday.org) has called for a "Time to Care" legislative agenda for the United States, including paid family leave, paid sick leave, three weeks of paid vacation, limits on compulsory overtime and policies making it easier to choose part-time work with healthcare and other benefits.

increasing access to part-time work. Ellen Galinsky, President and co-founder of the Families and Work Institute, notes that in order for there to be more part-time work options, "As a country we have to solve the health issue. I don't see solving the part-time issue without also addressing the issue of healthcare, but that said, when employers recognize that they get a lot more from part-time workers then that might change the way they think."

Some companies actually "game" the system, purposefully using part-time labor so that they can avoid paying for benefits. For struggling families this may lead to parents having to work multiple part-time jobs in order to keep the telephone on, electricity running, and to pay medical bills. In this situation, there is little time to spare, not even for little family members. Quite obviously, this is not family-friendly part-time work.

Another common pitfall with part-time work is that employees often report being paid to work part-time, but then ending up working more hours per week than they are paid to do. One organization, the Center for WorkLife Law directed by Joan Williams, the same woman who inspired the owner of Johnson Moving and Storage, responded to this problem by working with employers and by sharing the benefits of family-friendly policies, concentrating on one professional sector (attorneys). Through these efforts, the Center for WorkLife Law prompted changes in part-time work situations for lawyers with their Project for Attorney Retention (PAR) program.

The Center for WorkLife Law reports that "In Washington, D.C., where PAR began, law firms have virtually eliminated the 'haircut' (e.g. 60 percent salary for an 80 percent schedule). PAR has also been effective in discouraging the practice, formerly widespread in D.C., of taking part-timers off the partnership track, and has witnessed a marked increase in the number of male lawyers working part-time—a sure sign that part-time schedules are becoming less stigmatized."[29] Many lawyers have used the PAR resources to institute similar changes in other parts of the country.

Part-time work options can benefit employers as well as employees. "Our research shows that if people are dual-focused, which means they prioritize work, as well as other things, then they are reenergized for work," says Ellen Galinsky, President and co-founder of the Families and Work Institute. "People who work part-time often have more energy than others."

Additional research backs up Galinsky's assessment that part-time workers often excel in their positions: The authors of *Beyond Work-Family Balance* write, "Our research indicates that making this connection [between the 'public sphere of paid work and the private sphere of personal life'], particularly at the level of work practices, can produce significant improvements in people's lives and in workplace performance."[30] And several real-world analysis of businesses as they institute flexible work policies, in particular at Deloitte and Dupont, have found that businesses benefit when they offer part-time and flexible work in a way that doesn't bar career advancement because it significantly improves employee retention.[31]

Liz was able to keep the same pro-rated pay and benefits when she went back to work part-time, and the part-time attorneys in Washington, D.C., are in much better situations thanks to the Center for WorkLife Law efforts. Yet clearly, this is not the norm. In fact, equitably paid part-time work with any form of benefits is often very difficult to find, leaving this option open to few parents. In order to allow parents to work part-time so they can better balance work and family, not only do more part-time jobs need to be offered, but employers need to stop penalizing part-time workers and pay them the same hourly rate, including pro-rata benefits, as similar full-time jobs.

Some countries have already embraced making part-time work available to all who request it. The Netherlands, for example, which has the highest percentage of part-time workers

(44 percent) of any country in the world,[32] has passed laws to make sure part- and full-time workers are treated equally.[33]

"We are in a transition between the twentieth century workplace with an industrial economy, and a twenty-first century workplace. The industrial economy required a one-size-fits-all workplace. In the transition we are in now, the nature of work, the economy, and the nature of the workforce are very different. In the past, part-time work was seen as a lesser kind of work, looking at the horizon we are going to think of new ways to work that work for both the employee and employer," says Galinsky noting that increased access to flexible work options, including part-time work, is part of what's on the horizon.

As Liz went back to work she found that she also had to make adjustments with her husband on the home front, since work done at home is part of the overall work equation. Early on, after spending her day at the office, Liz was up late one evening making her then eighteen-month-old son lunch for the next day as her husband relaxed on the couch in the living room with a book. "I was feeling a little bitter," recalls Liz. "I said, 'This work isn't done yet, I need some help here, please get off the couch because I would like to be reading too.'" It was a breakthrough moment for her husband. "Something clicked in his brain. He realized it wasn't a 'Brian repairs things in the house and Liz does all the shopping, cleaning, and laundry' situation; but that we both contribute what we can until all the work is done in a given night."

Because of more equal treatment at home and a progressive

and accommodating workplace, Liz has realized self-proclaimed "domestic bliss," enjoying both of her jobs. "I'm totally satisfied with my work and home balance."

Part-time work is an effective answer for many women who would find flexible full-time (or more) work like Dr. Stone's too intensive. But while Liz is an example of what can go well with part-time work arrangements, it remains that the majority of part-time workers aren't faring as well. In order to make part-time work a viable option for American workers with families, the following steps must be taken:

- Part-time workers should receive equitably pro-rated pay in relation to similar employees in full-time positions.
- Part-time positions need to be more widely available, as well as structured into a broad cross-section of jobs to alleviate tension between full- and part-time employees.
- Those who work part-time should not be held back from promotions.
- Part-time workers should be paid for all the hours they work and not be pushed to work past their scheduled hours without compensation.
- Part-time workers should receive some form of benefits.

With these changes, we can go a long way toward making part-time work equitably compensated and a viable reality for many American families.

Sequencing

Martha was away from her home, yet again traveling on a business trip. Seven months pregnant with her second child, she was sitting in the waiting area of a small Horizon Airlines terminal in the Portland airport when she suddenly got a creepy feeling. She just had to know what her two-year-old son, at home with their nanny, was doing at that very moment. Martha's son, like 10 percent of all children in childcare, was cared for at home by a nanny or babysitter.[34]

While waiting for her airplane, "I had this really unsettling feeling, which wasn't common for me," recalls Martha. So she called her father who lived close to her home and asked him to drive by her house to see what was going on with her son and the nanny on "one of those surprise visits that you read about in parenting magazines."

Her cell phone started ringing as Martha was walking across the tarmac to the rolling metal stairs that led into the airplane. It was her dad reporting back. After driving over to Martha's house, he found her son playing in the caregiver's parked car in the street while she was busy cleaning out her car. He wasn't pleased with what he saw, and neither was Martha. Not a capital offense, but not exactly what Martha imagined as ideal for her son's upbringing.

She made a huge decision right then about her next life steps as she talked on her cell phone while hovering under the airplane wing. The wind was whipping her hair into a tangled mess. "I felt like, 'That's it. I'm doing all this work to pay for my kid to play in a parked car in the street.' I felt like there were so many better things for him to be doing. So that's when I decided I needed to be more involved."

She explains that her problem wasn't so much about the caregiver, and notes that a lot of people wouldn't have a problem with what the caregiver was doing, but it was more that, "I wanted to be making those choices," she says, about what her son was doing each day.

So Martha quit her position as a vice president of a Fortune 500 company and decided to stay home for several years with her two children. Martha is one of many parents who are "sequencing," moving in and out of the workplace to care for children.

For the first time in twenty-five years, a growing number of women are taking time out of the workforce when they have infants (babies under a year old). In fact, the proportion of mothers of infants in the workforce declined from a record high of 59 percent in 1998, to a lower 55 percent in 2000. This was the first significant decline since the U.S. Census Bureau began publishing this statistic in 1976.[35] The decline continued in 2002, when 54.6 percent of mothers with infants were in the workforce.[36]

That said, 72 percent of all mothers with children over one year old were in the labor force.[37] What does this mean? It means that more women are leaving their jobs to stay home with babies for the first year of their child's life, but that women aren't opting out of work completely; they are going back to work when their children are older.

Having babies is a happy reality of life, and many parents savor the time spent away from work caring for a new baby. The problem with parents quitting their jobs to stay home with a newborn is that mothers, and families, suffer long-lasting financial consequences when they leave the workforce. Yet, without flexible work options, and without long-term paid family leave, quitting their jobs is the best option many parents have available to them. Ideally, work structures should be set up to allow parents to work around the ebb and flow of family needs and to also enjoy time with their children. But right now they're not.

Because of this, many new mothers don't have a real "choice" about whether or not to quit their jobs. If they didn't have a high paying job to start or access to paid family leave, many women find the cost of infant childcare would eat their entire paycheck. For these mothers, taking time out of the workforce, or sequencing, may be the most practical option, particularly if a relative or some other person isn't available to watch their infant for free while they work.

For many women, being a full-time parent isn't an option because their paycheck is needed to support the family; and many families with a full-time parent at home are struggling. One clear indication of this is that families with a stay-at-home parent are seven times more likely to live in poverty than those with two working parents.[38] In fact, the birth of a child is too often a time of extreme financial challenge for American families, with a quarter of "poverty spells" starting with the birth of a baby.[39]

One thing all mothers who take time out of the workforce have in common is they will all take long-lasting wage hits, or pay cuts, when they later return to the workforce (and, remember, wage hits have been tied to our lack of family friendly policies). The beginning of this chapter discussed the wage hits mothers take when they leave the workforce, but didn't discuss how long those wage hits continue into the future.

Those wage hits, it turns out, persist for decades after returning to the workforce. The biggest decline in wages is seen during the first year back to work; though the wage gap does narrow the longer women are back in the workplace, more than two decades later these women still make far less than their counterparts who kept working without breaks.[40] One notable study published in the *Monthly Labor Review*, reports, "Women whose gaps [time out of the workplace] ended less than one year ago had wages that were 33 percent lower than those of women who did not leave the labor force. By the third year (when they would have returned to the work force more than three years ago) these women's wages were only 20 percent lower than those of women who remained in the labor force."[41]

Contrary to the authors of the study, we think "only" 20 percent lower wages after three years back in the labor force is an eye-catching and depressing statistic for all women. What's more, the gap never completely disappears, regardless of the time back at work. The report continues, "Even women whose labor force gap occurred more than twenty years ago still earn between

5 and 7 percent less than women who never left the labor force and have comparable levels of experience."[42]

One of the biggest long-term costs of sequencing is women's increased risk for having inadequate retirement income. Our retirement system is based on earnings, so full-time parents don't accrue social security or other retirement benefits during their time at home. Retirement benefits also rarely transfer from job to job. In fact, women account for a disproportionate, and growing, percentage of the elderly poor. In 1983 women made up 71 percent of seniors living below the poverty line; in 1995 it was 75 percent.

It's clear that despite the short- and long-term economic hits, more women are moving in and out of the labor force after the birth of a child. Some are sequencing quite successfully.

A pioneer in successful sequencing, former U.S. Secretary of State Madeleine Albright went back to paid work after fifteen years of juggling parenting and graduate school. She recalls an incident indicative of her life then. "I was working for U.S. Senator Muskie and my youngest daughter, Katie [then seven], called for me on the phone." Katie was told, " 'I'm sorry, you can't talk to your mom right now. She's on the floor with Senator Muskie.' " Secretary Albright clearly relishes recounting the punch line, "When I got home my daughter said, 'Mom, I know you have a new job, but what were you doing on the floor with Senator Muskie!?' " The floor, of course, was the voting area of the United States Senate. Not quite the picture her daughter had in mind.

Whether or not one agrees with Secretary Albright's politics, there's no question she's a formidable woman. Secretary Albright served as the U.S. permanent representative to the United Nations; as a member of President Clinton's cabinet; as a staff member on the National Security Council; and most recently, was the first woman in the history of the U.S. government to achieve the high rank of U.S. secretary of state, fourth in line to the president.

She is also a former full-time mom who didn't get started in her current professional career until she was thirty-nine.

"People find it hard to believe that I was home with my children. It wasn't until I went into the Clinton administration that my chronological age and my professional age matched, because I had 'taken time out,' " says Secretary Albright, discussing the time spent with her children.[45]

Mothers like Secretary Albright show it's possible to high jump over the "maternal wall." But individual success stories don't translate into widespread success for women. The maternal wall is holding strong. As this chapter reveals, studies show the majority of mothers suffer the long-term economic burdens of motherhood, which increase with employment breaks, for their entire lives.

One way many women deal with inflexible work environments when "sequencing" in and out of the workforce is to take working matters into their own hands. Many moms who quit work when they had children, later create their own flexible work arrangements when they sequence back into the workforce by starting their own businesses. In fact, women are starting businesses at more than double the rate of the general American public.[46]

Martha, the mother under the airplane wing, is one such woman. After six years out of the labor force, she started her own public relations firm, noting, "I knew that when I went back to work it was going to have to wrap around my life and my family's life. I really want to see my kids when they are young, so I knew I was going to have to create my own work environment because I didn't see that possibility with my old employer—not to slam them, but it's a current reality of a very large workplace. They have their business and they want to run it their way, but that doesn't mean I have to run my business their way. I'm happy running mine my way—and I'm quite successful too."

The reality is that a number of factors are going to have to come together to lessen the penalties on moms who take time out from paid work to care for children. First, the underlying causes that force some women to quit their jobs in order to stay home with infants need to be addressed. Providing support to new parents, as most other countries do, in the form of realistic paid family leave is a good start (the average industrial country guarantees significantly more weeks of leave than the U.S. does).[47] Second, allowing women (and men) flexible work options that let work wrap around family needs will go a long way toward helping parents, and businesses, in America succeed.

Working It Out

Dr. Stone, Susan, Liz, and Martha are all doing well with both work and family. Their stories suggest the rich variety of possibilities that workers and workplaces are beginning to explore. An increasing number of businesses recognize the benefits of offering employees family-friendly work opportunities, yet it's fair to say that the majority of workplaces have yet to adopt these practices. History has proven again and again that change is rarely easy.

Change upsets established power structures; it creates uncertainty, and makes those pushing for change from management positions particularly vulnerable if the gambit isn't immediately successful. After all, very few managers get fired for following established company policy, while backing new directions ties supporters to the success or failure of those efforts. This is why it's important to share the success stories of flexible work arrangements—these stories allow employers and employees to see the substantial potential benefits of implementing new policies without undertaking the risk of being the first to try a new venture. Managers, and business owners, can use the success stories to bolster their efforts. And, more efforts are certainly needed.

Right now, flexible work options are often limited to people holding jobs with higher education and pay. Karen Kornbluh notes this fact in a New America Foundation report, and elaborates, "Many businesses are finding ways to give their most valued employees flexibility but, all too often, workers who need flexibility find themselves shunted into part-time, temporary, on-call, or contract jobs with reduced wages and career opportunities—and, often, no benefits."[48] In addition, "A full quarter of American workers are in these jobs. Only 15 percent of women and 12 percent of men in such jobs receive health insurance from their employers. "This is certainly not family-friendly.

So how do needed changes happen? Many of the success stories shared in this chapter came about because businesses or organizations determined it was in their best interest to create family-friendly work policies. Often the initial impetus for workplace change comes from an individual, or individuals who have a need, coupled with an open-minded manager who sees that the employee need is compatible with the business, or, even better, overlaps with a business opportunity.

For instance, the owner of Johnson Moving and Storage was motivated to make changes when he determined it was the right thing to do for families. He then investigated and developed options that wouldn't hurt his business, and soon came to realize that those options allowed him to attract top employees as well as retain those already on board. In fact, offering family friendly work structures has a tendency to reinvigorate the old-fashioned mutual respect between employer and employee, resulting in greater job satisfaction for all involved.

The business community is starting to take note of the forthcoming workplace changes and the need for increased workplace flexibility to keep our economy healthy. A March 2005 *Harvard Business Review* article comments, "market and economic factors, both cyclical and structural, are aligned in ways guaranteed to make talent constraints and skills shortages huge issues again." The article goes on to note, "There is a winning strategy. It

revolves around the retention and reattachment of highly qualified women," and later concludes, "To tap this all-important
resource, companies must understand the complexities of
women's nonlinear careers and be prepared to support rather
than punish those who take alternative routes."[49]

Flexible work options—including part-time jobs that pay a
fair wage—allow working mothers to continue along demanding
and challenging career paths, put food on the table, make vital
contributions to our economy, and be good parents. Ultimately
this is good for us all—our families and our businesses.

Manifesto Point "O"

*Mothers need flexibility at work so they can continue to work effec-
tively while raising a family. And they need the ability to exit and
enter the workforce without the huge pay cuts given to those considered on "the mommy track."*

ACTION: Mothers want—

    (1) Government incentives for flexible work options.

    (2) Fair wages and benefits for part-time positions.

    (3) Fair wages for mothers returning to the workforce.

To find out more, go to **www.MotherhoodManifesto.com.**

NOT YOUR FATHER'S UNION

by Anna Burger, Secretary-Treasurer, Service Employees
International Union (SEIU) and Chair Change to Win

It's not just your father's union anymore. In fact, it's probably your mother's, or sister's, or daughter's.

Women are a higher percentage of union members now than anytime in American history, making a difference in their lives and in our society as a whole.

Just as the work force and workplace changed, unions are changing too and so have their priorities. No longer is it just about wages and benefits—now it's much broader, from childcare to comp time—helping women with the tools they need as they juggle work and family.

As a mother, and as a top officer of America's fastest growing union, I see that the changes happening in the workplace are having a profound impact on women's ability to balance work life and family life. And while union evolution has brought about several advancements, we have only begun to respond to the astonishing changes in our economy.

When I was a kid growing up in Pennsylvania, the daughter of a disabled truck driver and a nurse, a strong union movement made it possible for my brother and sisters and I to have a decent way of life. My parents were able to own their own home, and I was able to go to college, thanks to a higher prevalence of union jobs and the better standard of living they represent. Then, one in three workers was part of a union. Now, it's one in twelve. And working families like the one I grew up in are having to choose between sending their kids to school or paying for healthcare; buying gas or paying their rent.

My union, the Service Employees International Union (SEIU), is leading the way in using union power to help workers adjust to these changes. The majority of SEIU members are women, and they know full well the difficulty in juggling work and family demands in a difficult economic situation.

We are, in essence, recreating the entire workplace landscape. Once simply an employer-employee relationship, union members are now negotiating on behalf of their entire families, making a difference not only in their lives but in their communities.

Union members now seek benefits that deal with the meshing of work and family life. Parental leave, sick leave banks, comp time, and flextime are common in SEIU contracts. But that's not all. Workers are creating new rights that address real-life family and community needs.

- SEIU nurses have negotiated limits on mandatory overtime, a common hospital practice that wreaks havoc on nurses' family lives and puts patient safety at risk.
- SEIU members have won the right to use paid leave to attend parent/teacher conferences and other school-related activities with their children.
- SEIU members worked with employers to provide a wide range of childcare, recreation, education, and special needs funding for more than 10,000 children in New York.
- Last year in California, SEIU women members led a coalition that won unprecedented legislation providing better levels of paid maternity and paternity leave and flexible work and family programs.
- Hundreds of thousands of janitors, home care workers, nursing home employees, and others have access to affordable health insurance today simply because they formed a union with SEIU.
- And in changing work environments like home based childcare, our union is creating new models of unions to give working families a voice and improve their lives and the services they provide.

But even with these hard-won victories, more and more workers are without healthcare, pensions, or other benefits. Two things must happen to reverse this trend: One, unions must replicate on a mass scale the strategies described above, and two, unions must launch dramatic new organizing campaigns to bring millions more workers into the union fold.

Progressive change has never happened in our country from the top down. Uniting workers to have a real voice in their jobs will ensure that progress happens from the workplace up.

4

TV We Choose and Other After-School Programs

Every Tuesday night at 8 P.M. Ellen's entire family gathers around the television in their living room to watch the *Gilmore Girls*. It starts with one person figuring out that it is almost 8 P.M. and Tuesday. Then the rest of the family members are found in their various locations around the house and urged into the living room. Their dog, Riley, also joins the group and lies by the stairs—as long he's with his "pack," he's happy.

Ellen and her two children, Melissa, eleven years old, and Nate, fifteen years old, fit snugly onto one green over-stuffed couch that was once Ellen's grandmother's, while Denis, the dad, stretches out on a cozy floral patterned love seat—his feet resting on one arm of the love seat and head on the other.

With ever-increasing television and electronic entertainment options, many parents feel they can't fully escape the media onslaught. Some parents focus on teaching their children media literacy so kids learn how to determine what is appropriate on their own. Ellen and her family enjoy hanging out, having fun, and bantering back and forth when they watch television together.

This weekly gathering not only brings the family closely together, literally by sharing the same physical space, but also gives them a common story to discuss and an opportunity to exchange ideas about values. It also gives the family time to share some laughs, and, to sing—Ellen and Melissa regularly belt out the lyrics to the opening song and sometimes they even dance to the tunes of the more "happening" commercials during breaks in the show.

A few recent episodes had a storyline where the very close mother and daughter became estranged because of a major disagreement about the direction of the daughter's life. The two characters don't talk for several episodes, causing Ellen and her family to talk about relationships and what they would do in this case. Ellen comments, "The interesting thing is my daughter makes resolutions to not do this or not do that when she's older while she's watching the show. There's a real value to watching this type of show and thinking about the ramifications of different actions, particularly because most things in life aren't black and white. Watching this show together is an opportunity to get a little distance from daily human experiences, see both sides of issues, and then discuss how we would deal with the situation."

Most of these conversations occur after the show is over, or are quick comments during commercials, and every now and then it brings a moment where the family can talk together about deeper values. These discussions are part of the way they watch television, it's a natural and ongoing dialogue that uses a television program as a jumping off point for thinking about real-life choices.

One such jumping off point for Ellen came in the car on the way to the dentist. As Ellen and her son Nate, then thirteen, were winding down the residential roads of their neighborhood to a regular dental appointment, the topic of sex and romance came up. They had just watched a *Gilmore Girls* show where an intimate romance developed quite quickly, as they do in most shows, in order to keep the plot moving forward. Ellen used the topic of the show to talk about our culture's tendency to use sex for marketing purposes, to imply that everyone "cool" is doing it, and to emphasize that the standard whirlwind television romances are a fantasy norm far from reality. "Of course, he knew all this already because he's a teenager, but it still needs to be said by me, his mother," she recalls. "This was essentially the 'sex talk,' but

TEN COMMONSENSE MEDIA BELIEFS

By Common Sense Media (www.commonsensemedia.org)

1. We believe in media sanity, not censorship.
2. We believe that media has truly become "the other parent" in our kids' lives powerfully affecting their mental, physical, and social development.
3. We believe in teaching our kids to be savvy media interpreters—we can't cover their eyes but we can teach them to see.
4. We believe parents should have a choice and a voice about the media our kids consume. Every family is different, but all need information.
5. We believe that the price for a free and open media is a bit of extra homework for families. Parents need to know before they go.

not the talk about the mechanics; rather it was about the deeper emotional aspects of what sex is about. I wanted to be very clear about my core beliefs."

Television can be used to teach children critical thinking, discuss taboo subjects, as well as share and debate core values when parents and their children watch together. A key problem is that keeping the television on past the time of productive learning is so seductive. It can be downright addictive. Carl Bromley, the editor of *Cinema Nation,* puts it this way, "Like drinking good wine, if you drink too much of it then it doesn't matter how splendid the grape or aroma. It's bad for you psychologically." Too much of anything isn't good, and over indulging in television can suck valuable time away from other important activities. Yet it's so easy to do.

Ellen deals with this problem in her household, "Once you're watching television there's a strong momentum to watch the next

6. We believe that through informed decision making, we can improve the media landscape one decision at a time.
7. We believe appropriate regulations about right time, right place, right manner exist. They just need to be upheld by our elected and appointed leaders.
8. We believe in age-ppropriate media and that the media industry needs to act responsibly as it creates and markets media age-appropriate contents.
9. We believe there should be one, independent and transparent universal rating system for all media.
10. We believe in diversity of programming and media ownership.

show. So it takes discipline on my part to say, 'No.' Television is very much an impulse entertainment. It's very tempting, and is designed to be very tempting, and sometimes it's the right thing and sometimes it's not."

The other seductive aspect of television, in addition to the actual programming, is the commercials. The American Academy of Pediatrics reports that children see an average of 40,000 commercials per year.[1] Food and beverage advertisers alone spend between $10 billion and $12 billion per year advertising to kids through television commercials, special promotions, as well as targeted packaging and public relations.[2] Children are often easily taken in by these commercials: One study on the impact of media advertising to children found that when a toy advertisement was shown at the beginning and end of a preschool program, the majority of kids (70 percent) said they'd rather play with that toy than a friend.[3] Another study found that the more television children watched, the more they tried to get their parents to buy products while shopping.[4] Advertising is clearly influential.

Just as there are negative repercussions from spending too much time zoning out in front of the television, there are positive impacts from good educational programming. In fact, studies show that good educational programming, like *Sesame Street, Blue's Clues, Dora the Explorer, Arthur, Clifford,* and *Dragontales,* can help kids learn and can even show positive academic effects later in high school.[5] The key to successfully navigating television, many experts say, is to stay engaged with children and teach them critical thinking skills.

One of the biggest problems with television is that due to the nature of contemporary society, with many kids home alone after school because both parents are working, television has become a de facto parent. Liz Perle, Editor-in-Chief of Common Sense Media, comments on the present state of media in America, "The number one thing about media is, 'Who's raising your kid?' What you need to teach your kids now is not just what you believe and how that stacks up to stereotypes present in all media, but also how to be savvy media consumers. Every family has a choice about media and can be active or passive about how they engage in it." Taking time to watch television with children, and then discussing what is good and bad about the content, can be a learning experience children carry with them into the future.

The Media Diet

Kids are consuming a growing amount of media. There are two separate concerns about this trend: First, too much time in front of the television can leave little time for other activities. Second, the content of some television programming can be inappropriate, studies show sometimes harmful, for young viewers, and parents have too few tools available to determine television program content in advance.

On the first matter, a 2005 Kaiser Family Foundation report found that in the last five years the time young people spend exposed to media content each day (television, video games, DVDs, online, and music) has increased by more than an hour, to a total of eight hours and thirty-three minutes.[6] This same study found that each day the average American young person spends the following amount of time with these top entertainment sources: three hours and fifty-one minutes of television and videos; forty-eight minutes online; forty-nine minutes playing video games; and one hour and forty-four minutes listening to music.[7] This is per day, not per week, and shows a huge steady media diet.

The content in this media diet is troubling: By the time the average child gets to elementary school they will have viewed 8,000 murders and 100,000 acts of violence on television.[8] More troubling, the representation of violence is often overstylized, gung ho, and cartoonish, lacking both a strong moral and realistic foundation in much of American programming. Storytelling is reduced to a series of showy violent set pieces where character development is minimal. As Todd Gitlin, a professor of journalism and sociology at Columbia University, observed, "TV versions of violence are egregious, coarsening, and produce a social fear and anesthesia which damage our capacity to face reality."[9] But does exposure to television violence trigger real-life violence? It's a debate that has raged for decades.

Some use the example of Japan to argue that exposure to televised violence doesn't trigger real-life violence. This is because, as Todd Gitlin notes, "There is far more vile media violence—including more widely available violent pornography—in Japan than in the United States." Yet Japan has a much lower rate of violent criminal offenses than we have in the United States. This information calls for a factual double take: Why the connection with increased violence here and not there? Something must be off, no?

Looking closely it's clear that not only are there significant cultural differences between the two countries; there are also differences in how televised violence is presented in Japan. "One study found that the portrayal of violence in Japan vastly differs from that in the United States," writes Dr. Eugene Beresin, Associate Professor of Psychiatry at the Harvard Medical School, in *Academic Psychiatry*. "In Japan the violence is more realistic, in that the pain and suffering associated with the violent act is emphasized. Also, the violence is mainly committed by the villain against the hero; therefore, acts of violence are associated with bad people and seen as inappropriate and immoral."[10] Clearly other factors are at play here.

The debate rages in communications circles, many arguing that culture and context of the media violence is a key factor in the impact on the viewer. "The [Japan] argument assumes that media violence is the only, or major and always decisive, influence on human and social behavior," suggests George Gerbner, former dean of the Annenberg School of Communication at the University of Pennsylvania. "Media violence (or any other single factor) is one of many factors interacting with other influences in any culture that contribute to real-world violence," he concludes.[11]

Here in the United States, researchers, led by Vincent P. Mathews, M.D., professor of radiology, at the Indiana School of Medicine, are gaining clarity that media violence does make an impact by reaffirming the connection between viewing violent media and increased violent behavior in a study released in June of 2005. This study concluded that exposure to media violence may alter brain function whether or not the viewer has had previous aggressive behavior. William Kronenberger, Ph.D., associate professor in the Department of Psychiatry, who collaborated on the study, was quoted saying, "There are myriad articles showing that exposure to violent TV especially causes individuals to be more aggressive. We are studying the neurological and self-control processes that underlie the aggressive behavior."[12]

Sexual media content is also increasing, and has been shown to

ADVERTISING CONCERNS AND ACTION

by Betsy Taylor, founder of the Center for a New American Dream

A majority of American parents say they want their children to watch less television, but even larger numbers worry about commercials and advertising. Kids ages two to eighteen watch an average of 40,000 television commercials a year.

Virtually from birth, today's children are exposed to banner ads, television commercials, logos and product placements. According to a poll by the Center for a New American Dream, 87 percent of parents say that advertising and marketing aimed at kids today make children and teenagers too materialistic. Between 1981 and 1997, American youth increased the time they spent on shopping by 50 percent.

be quite influential on kids' behavior. A study released in November of 2005 found that the number of sex scenes on television has nearly doubled since 1998, with 70 percent of 2005 shows including some sexual content.[13] There are important real-life implications to this increase in sexual content: Teens who regularly watch television shows with sexual content are significantly more likely to have sexual intercourse than those who do not.[14]

Kids also have increased access to television, and a tremendous number of children have a television in their bedroom (68 percent of eight to eighteen-year-olds)[15] where parents have little control over how much time children are spending watching television or what types of programs kids choose. Not surprisingly, kids with televisions in their bedrooms watch more by nearly an hour and a half per day, than those that don't. Many organizations advocate getting televisions out of kid's bedrooms

Parents are taking action. Here are a few tips for parenting in a commercial world:

- Limit your child's exposure to television and to commercial media, especially when children are young. Mute commercials when you do have family viewing.
- Talk to your child about advertising. Make a game of analyzing how a company is trying to "trick" your child into thinking he'll be cool if he just eats the right potato chips or buys a certain kind of fast food.
- When you say no to the nagging for another video game, overpriced sneaker, or expensive jeans, say yes to something your child really wants that money can't buy. Remember the magical moments from your own childhood and try to claim them for your own children. Turn off the television and ride a bike, bake a pie, visit some cousins, or get up a game of capture the flag. Consider this motto: More fun, less stuff.

and into a public place in the home so families can decide both content and time issues together.[16]

Studies show that television content can have a big impact on children's behavior, and the consequences of children viewing glamorized sexual and violent content that is devoid of any real-world context on television is undoubtedly something parents, communities, and governments shouldn't overlook. There is substantial controversy about where to draw lines for appropriate content in broadcast television. No matter where that line gets drawn, it is possible to find common ground that gives parents the ability to choose what is appropriate for their own homes and for their children to view.

Children, however, still need guidance. It's important to set a healthy media diet for children—adult supervision and media content discussions, setting limits to TV viewing time, taking the time to choose appropriate programming, utilizing technologies like the V-chip and lock boxes, taking TVs out of kids' bedrooms, or even the old fashioned "Off" button are needed to do so.

As a community we need to insist on the consistent enforcement of reasonable Federal Communications Commission (FCC) regulations that allow parents to choose what is showing in their own homes. The FCC doesn't have consistent standards that are easy for television broadcasters to understand and, by many accounts inconsistently enforces regulations. This is troublesome because parents need accurate information in order to make informed decisions about television viewing. If something is rated TV-G (general audiences), then the program should consistently have TV-G content.

The FCC needs to provide clarity on their regulations, including clarifying reasonable place, time, and manner restrictions, so parents can make educated selections. The bottom line is there are no clear standards. (It should be noted that the FCC has quite different regulations for cable content than television broadcasters. This is mainly because the FCC licenses television broadcast companies to use the public airways, while cable companies send their programming over privately owned and maintained cables.)

Ultimately, children need to learn how to screen content on their own to become media literate adults. Perle notes that since media is a fact of life: "Children have to exercise their non-media muscles, but media literacy has to be placed along reading, writing, and arithmetic as an educational survival skill. It has to be up there as part of a twenty-first century education."

High-Tech Options for Parental Content Control

A Blue's Brothers poster, framed diplomas, awards, and bookshelves covered the beige walls of Tim Collings' office at Simon Fraser University in Canada where he taught engineering. He looked up from reviewing reports when someone came in and told Tim there had just been shootings at a similar engineering school, the Ecole Polytechnique in Montreal. It was December of 1989. Fourteen women were killed and thirteen women injured, after Marc Lepine, who was denied entrance to the school, went on a rampage with a semi-automatic rifle. The carnage ended when Lepine turned the gun on himself.

After hearing the news, Tim went in search of a television. He got up from his L-shaped desk, passed the wall of books, and walked into the main engineering lab. This big 5,000 square foot lab room was out his office door, and he walked though it—past tables full of various electrical equipment, including power supplies, electric oscilloscopes, and digital multimeters that people were using for research and development—and into a video conferencing room on other side of lab where there was a television. He was horrified as he watched the reports of the massacre.

The shootings deeply affected Tim, "It was a shocking thing you don't expect to happen—this man walked into a lecture room with a machine gun and at the end of the day there were

fourteen students killed and then he shot himself." Tim listened
to updates on the radio, watched the news, and later read reports.
Everyone was asking, "Why?" including Tim.

Then Tim read the report detailing the fact that searchers
found a library of violent video material in the murderer's apart-
ment. There were a number of news stories about connections
between increased violence and media consumption. Something
clicked for Tim.

As an engineer and inventor, Tim knew how to bring ideas
into reality. "If you're an inventor you come across problems
every day and start thinking about solutions—this thing popped
out to me as a problem," recalls Tim. Tim figured there are two
ways to help stem the tide of increasingly violent media into
homes: The first is censorship that eliminates violence at the
source. The second lets the viewers decide what they allow into
their homes. Tim took the second approach.

Figuring out that broadcasters could include age-appropriate
rating information in television transmissions (in the same way
close caption text for the hearing impaired was already included);
he developed a device to receive these program rating codes that
could be built into television sets and act as a filter based on user
preference. This idea turned into the V-chip. It took Tim about
six months to develop a prototype and over a decade to deal with
corporate and government policies to get the rating and filtering
system up and running.

Tim's invention from Canada is closely tied to the United

States because, as he says, "We passed similar regulations in Canada, but the consumer electronics association which is the umbrella organization that coordinates television manufacturers has headquarters in Washington, D.C. So if you want to deal with the television manufacturers then you have to go through D.C. because North America is really one entity, and most products that get into Canada go through the United States."

Dealing with the manufacturers was essential in order to get the V-chip integrated into each newly made television. Tim comments, "The FCC in the United States has a lot more clout and when they put legislation in place that restricts the sale of televisions without V-chips then it really has to happen." His strategy was that if he could get the FCC to require V-chips in televisions, then the television manufacturers and broadcasters would use the same systems in Canada. His strategy paid off. By lobbying the United States Congress and FCC he was able to pass requirements for the V-chip system that were also implemented in his home country.

V-chips are now incorporated into all new televisions manufactured since 2000.[17] The television program rating system from which the V-chip gets its information is also up and running. Federal law now mandates that almost all television shows are rated so the viewing public can determine what they want showing in their homes. The ratings designations are: TV-Y (all children); TV-Y7 (age 7 and above); TV-G (general audience); TV-PG (parental guidance suggested); TV-14 (parents strongly

cautioned); TV-MA (mature audiences only).[18] These designations can be used with the V-chip as a filter, or to select appropriate programming in real time.[19]

There is a high degree of consumer confusion about media
rating designations. With different rating systems for television,
video games, movies, and other media this isn't surprising. A
Kaiser Family Foundation survey found very few parents of
young children, less than half of those surveyed, understand the
television ratings for their child's age group (TV-Y7 and TV-Y).
And even fewer parents understand the content-based rating
designations: Only 5 percent knew the D rating was for sugges-
tive dialogue, while 62 percent knew V is for violence.[20] On top
of this problem is the fact that many of the ratings for individual
programs are inaccurate: A University of California at Los
Angeles School of Public Health study published in May of 2005
found the number of violent acts in a movie wasn't always correlated with the rating the movie was given.[21] Clearly we need an
independent uniform rating system with consistent content cate-
gories that crosses all media to avoid parental confusion and
allow better consumer choices.

Another important issue is that very few people know they
have a high tech content controlling tool, the V-chip, in their
household. A survey in 2001 found that while 40 percent of families owned a television with a V-chip, only 17 percent were actually using it. This is, in part, because most families with V-chips
in their televisions don't even know they have one (53 percent).

Of those that do know, substantially less than half use it.[22] Educating more parents how to use the V-chip can help parents control what's showing in their living rooms.

Tim notes that the V-chip is fairly easy to use with a regular remote control. "You don't need anything special. Take your remote control and use the menu button. If you push the menu button then you'll see a number of different controls—in most sets, all new sets now, there is selection for parental controls and those controls at the minimum will allow you to set certain ratings, and some also have channel blocking and time allowances."

New technologies like the V-chip give parents some ability to control the television content shown in their own homes. Other devices that allow parents to choose the programs available to their children include lock boxes, which are available from cable companies and allow people to lock out unwanted channels, and digital set-top boxes, which often have increased abilities to block programs based on information like ratings, program titles, and time.[23]

Another way for individuals to control the television programming available in their homes is to allow people to simply pay for the channels they want to watch, and not pay for those they would have blocked. Many people call this "a la carte" program selection, or unbundling cable packages. Right now, people generally buy cable packages that come with several preselected channels together in one bundle. There is a movement to "unbundle" cable packages, i.e. allow people to buy only the channels they want in an a la carte fashion. While this option has been proposed by a wide variety of groups, from liberal-leaning consumer groups to conservative decency groups, it's not yet available to consumers.

In 2004, U.S. Senator John McCain sponsored a bill that would have forced cable companies to have a la carte options available. Consumers still could buy bundled packages, but the option would be there for purchasing individual channels. The a la carte option is remarkably simple for consumers, but it's rife with controversy mainly because cable companies are worried about how it will impact their bottom line. For this, and a number of other reasons, the 2004 effort failed.

Activists remain interested in continuing forward on this path, however. Josh Silver, Executive Director of Free Press, notes, "The real goal of a la carte is to ensure people, not cable companies, can decide what channels they receive and pay for in their homes. This is important because 98 percent of people in the U.S. only have the choice of one cable provider in the area, mainly because cable companies are inherently monopolistic due to the nature of the technology."

Tim agrees that unbundling cable channels, or a la carte options, are part of the wave of the future. "It only makes sense for the industry to go that way at one point." And, he notes, "The big future is IP (internet protocol) television where everything goes over the internet so your cable company or phone company would now be able to distribute video programming over the same connection. This will involve a more targeted reception of programming because there will be millions of program options that aren't time based. There could still be V-chip type codes in the data to help sort."

Often though, the time spent watching TV is more of a problem than the content. A fairly simple solution to both those issues is to simply turn off the television and do something else.

Turning Off the Television and Getting Active

Lucas was fifteen and at loose ends. He wandered over to the local Boys and Girls Club after school was out a few times and played basketball on their outdoor court. He wasn't thrilled with shooting and dribbling around outside. It just wasn't that much fun. Then one day he ventured into the building to play basketball on the indoor court, and his life turned around.

He was standing at the double doors between the lobby and outside, about to leave the Club for the day, when a staff person, Mike, tapped him on the shoulder and said, "Can I help you?"

Lucas responded, "No, I'm just going to take off." Mike continued, "What's your name?"

They introduced themselves, and then Mike asked Lucas, "Do you want to meet some people?"

Lucas responded, "Not really." But Mike further explained to Lucas that the "people" were teenagers and Lucas responded, "Oh really, well I could do that."

Matt led Lucas to the Teen Room at the Boys and Girls Club.

As Lucas walked into the teen room, which had teen drawings and artwork plastered all over the walls, he saw a whole bunch of teens hanging out, and knew he found a fun place to be after school. "In the teen room there were guitars and magic cards, talking, break dancing, listening to music, regular cards, just hanging out. Two doors open right off into the gym so we could always go out and play basketball. There was always an adult teen director back there with you so things didn't get out of hand," recalls Lucas.

From then on Lucas started hanging out at the Boys and Girls Club after school. At first he mainly hung out with other teens and had fun. He loved listening to music, playing on the computer, and playing the guitar. Then one day one of the Sports Directors, Neal, pulled Lucas aside and asked if he could help coach a baseball team of ten- and twelve-year-old boys.

Lucas pitched in. Seeing he was doing well, Mike, the Team Director started getting Lucas more involved in the Keystone program, a high school community service program that does a wide variety of activities including tutoring students, setting up community events like car washes, and helping organize Teen Dance Nights every other Friday.

This is when Lucas' life really started to change for the better, "I was tutoring younger kids, and from doing that it motivated me to do better. I was telling all these kids to work better and harder, but I wasn't doing it myself so I figured I'd be a role model," recalls Lucas. He continues, "Honestly I don't think I would have graduated from high school. When I got there in ninth grade I wasn't taking my studies very seriously. I slowly started taking my studies more seriously and ended up in the Running Start program where I started college in my senior year of high school."

The Boys and Girls Club that Lucas attended has an Education Director who caters to up to fifty kids a week for tutoring, and regularly sets up times with older students or volunteers to work more extensively with a young child to give them extra academic help. They also have a "Power Hour" from 4 P.M. until 5 P.M. every weekday, which is a time when every kid in system does homework. After that it's back to activities, fun, and games.

This after school program made a huge difference in Lucas's life, he says, because, "I was spending every afternoon at the Club. It was a place of belonging and really was a second family." Lucas lives with his mom, and she has to work full-time to support them both. She can't be around after school.

Before Lucas found the Boys and Girls Club, he was home alone until 6 P.M. or 7 P.M. every weeknight, and he'd been doing this since about the fifth grade. "It's hard to just be alone all the time. If I weren't at the Boys and Girls Club I would be home—not doing homework, but playing video games, playing with my dogs, or watching movies."

Studies show kids who go to formal after school programs watch less television, and have higher academic achievement as well as better social adjustment.[24] These advantages, combined with the fact that the peak time for juvenile crime is right after school gets out,[25] makes a compelling case for after school care options.

Communities are dealing with the need for after school care in many different ways. Several national organizations with local chapters have stepped up to the plate, including the Boys and Girls Club and the YMCA. Many public schools provide after school curriculum and enhancement, as do some private schools. Often local churches and other nonprofit organizations step in to fill the void in after school programs in communities across America. Yet while there are countless creative ways communities are reaching out to children in the late afternoon hours, there still aren't enough programs.

Right now, too few children have after school care. More than 40,000 kindergarteners are home alone after school, with a total of more than 14,000,000 kindergarteners through twelfth grade kids on their own after school without supervision.[26]

"The reality is that most parents work. So kids need a place to go after school where they are safe and stimulated," says Jodi Grant, Executive Director of the After School Alliance. "The truth is that even for families that have one parent at home, after school programs build social and other skills that they don't learn during the day." She comments that skills involving team work, dancing, drama, arts and crafts, physical fitness, and music are often highlighted in after school programs in ways that they can't be during the school day.

Grant notes that after school programs can be crucial, "For most kids, after school care is an opportunity to get one-on-one mentoring and run around, but for at-risk kids after school programs can literally be the difference between graduating and jail."

Providing after school care to at-risk youth not only benefits kids, but also the community coffers. A study of the effects of the After School Education and Safety Program Act of 2002 found that every dollar spent on an at-risk youth in an after school program brings a return of $8.92 to $12.90, mainly due to the amount saved by channeling the at-risk youth away from a life of crime (remember the juvenile crime rate is highest in the hours after school). Providing after school programs to nonrisk youth also brings a return (between $2.99 and $4.05 for every dollar spent) due to, in part, improved school performance and graduation rates.[27]

There are other ways after school programs can benefit children: Combating the epidemic of childhood obesity is one. University of Otago, New Zealand, researchers recently confirmed the connection between television and obesity, and further added to the data by finding that time spent watching television was a greater predictor of future obesity than diet or exercise.[28]

After school programs provide a different way for kids to spend their time than sitting in front of a television or other sedentary entertainment. "There's new focus, rightly so, on childhood obesity and the fact that kids going home and plopping on the couch, possibly with chips, can contribute to that problem," says Grant. "They can instead go and run around in an after school programs."

Designing a Better Program

Exposure to countless hours of mindless entertainment is particularly harmful during our children's formative years. By assuming greater control of what we show in our own homes and increasing funding for after school programs, we can limit that negative exposure and offer positive alternatives with real benefits for our children's wellbeing.

Parents are not without tools to help control the programming they allow their children to see, but the tools are insufficient compared to the flood of entertainment. Parents need help. They simply can't do it alone. Unbundling cable channels so families can buy what they want to watch on their televisions and keep out what they don't; setting a clear and consistent universal rating system for all forms of media; educating parents about how to use the technological controls available to them like the V-chip and lock-boxes; advocating that the FCC use its power to make sure content complies with the laws on the books and give better clarity about broadcasting standards; and working to ensure after school programs are funded and accessible are all important goals to work toward.

The violence, risky sexual behavior, and general bad modeling shown regularly on television come with a cost: Our youth are being taught life choices by stunt models and digital characters without any links to reality. The many channels of modern media have, to some degree, replaced the human community that used to nurture children. There is a fundamental need for mature adult guidance in an increasingly complex world. Investing in children now by giving their parents the tools they need to guide their children's media consumption, and providing programs that connect youth to purposeful activities that inform their lives is something we as a society cannot afford to neglect.

Chapter "T" Manifesto Point:

Mothers are outraged by poor quality television programming because it's harming our children. Mothers need help guarding our kids from exploitive television. It's time for society to get serious about giving better options to kids who come home to an empty house after school. Moreover, mothers need after school programs to engage our kids in healthy and productive activities.

ACTION: Mothers want—

(1)   A clear and independent universal rating system for parents and families, and meaningful public funding for quality educational programming.

(2)   Unbundled, al la carte cable packages so consumers can buy just the channels they want, and easy access to high tech devices for parents to better manage appropriate viewing in their own homes.

(3)   Increased access and funding for after school programs.

To get more informed, go to **www.MotherhoodManifesto.com.**

5

Healthcare for All Kids

Standing at her kitchen island, Lori opened an envelope and immediately started crying tears of relief. Just moments before, on a cold and rainy fall day, she reached into her black mailbox and pulled out a bundle of mail. She then turned and went back up her gravel drive into her house to separate the junk mail from bills and personal correspondence. One of the envelopes was from Children's Hospital.

Lori's daughter Haley spent a good part of her childhood at Children's Hospital. Right before Haley's second birthday, after

MISSING COVERAGE

Of the over seventy-seven million children in the United States, 12 percent don't have insurance coverage at all; 56 percent have health insurance through a parent's work; and 4 percent are covered by independent health insurance packages.[35]

painting her face red with lipstick in the wonderfully random fashion that only a toddler can pull off, Haley came down with a terrible rash. At first, doctors thought the rash was an irritation from the lipstick. Then Haley became unable to ride her tricycle or climb up the steps to her favorite slide.

Haley's muscle weakness was increasing, and the rash wasn't going away. The timing of the lipstick experiment and the rash turned out to be purely coincidental. Something far worse was going on. It was every family's worst nightmare: Lori's daughter Haley was gravely ill.

Haley was diagnosed with dermatomyositis, a complicated and sometimes deadly autoimmune disorder.

Lori is a full-time mother, and Haley's father, Layne, is self-employed. The family always made sure to purchase independent health insurance. But the packages available for self-employed people are "fairly expensive with lousy coverage," as Lori notes. Still, the family assumed Haley's care would be covered and were happy to see Haley responding well to treatment. Her disease even went into remission.

But when Haley was ten, she had a significant relapse of her disease. In short order, more than $120,000 of medical bills added up at Children's Hospital. The health insurance company found several loopholes in the family's insurance package and denied coverage for Haley's treatment. The family was stuck with the entire bill.

In Haley's case, although she had insurance through an independent healthcare package and the family thought they were fully covered, they soon found out otherwise. Her insurance turned out to be completely inadequate, which left her family vulnerable.

It was after this relapse that Lori opened the Children's Hospital letter. "I probably read the letter three or four times because it was one of those moments that makes you catch your breath because you can't believe what it says," remembers Lori.

MOMS WITHOUT COVERAGE

Women are starting their own businesses at more than double the rate of the overall population, with an increasing number getting independent healthcare packages.[36] As many mothers start their own businesses in order to have flexible work schedules, they are finding it difficult to get insurance because it is too expensive and/or inadequate.

The letter read: Based on your financial situation, Children's Hospital has agreed to pay, through the uncompensated care fund, all medical expenses your insurance doesn't cover.

In this case, with a bill over $120,000, the insurance wasn't covering anything. Had it not been for the extraordinary gift on the part of Children's Hospital, Lori and Layne may have faced bankruptcy.

"I immediately called the number at the bottom of the letter and I was really crying at this point because I just couldn't believe it. It's like the biggest burden had been lifted—it's so hard when your child is really sick, and then to have such enormous financial burdens is even worse. It was so amazing for it to just be lifted. It's hard to even describe what that was like," comments Lori.

Children's Hospital in Seattle, Washington, has the largest all-volunteer fundraising organization of any hospital in North America; in 2004, volunteers contributed over 90,000 hours to fundraising efforts and the hospital used thirty-five million dollars in the uncompensated care fund to aid families whose income or insurance coverage is limited.

Each year nearly 60 percent of patients at Children's Hospital—more than 57,000 children and teens—receive financial aid through Children's financial assistance program for uncompensated care. Haley was one of those 57,000 patients, and she, in theory at least, had insurance. Universal financial assistance for healthcare isn't available, most hospitals can't fill in the gaps to the degree that Children's Hospital in Seattle can, and as a result too many families are either forgoing needed care or ending up in bankruptcy.

Across our nation at least nine million children have no health insurance at all.[1] And because so many families are *under*insured, the statistics regarding children without adequate healthcare coverage are skewed; the real number is far greater than nine million. Only the very lucky few can win the healthcare lottery as Haley did.

Bankrupt Families

Zach's mom, Sharon, first had an inkling that something wasn't quite right with her son when he was three months old. Zach got bronchiolitis, an upper respiratory tract infection that inflames the small passageways in the lungs. "It was so bad, and lasted for so long. I mean he was sick for months," recalls Sharon.

But it wasn't until Zach was seven years old—after six years of regular doctor visits, countless surgeries, IV antibiotics, and months and months of oral antibiotics, as well as intestinal problems that at one point had him waking up every night to throw up—that it really became clear what was going on with him.

During those first several years of his life, Zach often ended up in the doctor's office at least once a week. Sharon and her family had health insurance that covered the entire family, but the co-pays, deductibles, and other costs added up. Sharon calculates that her family's out-of-pocket medical expenses each year ranged from as low as $14,000 to as high as $23,000 in 2004.

Sharon explains how this happened *even though they are covered by insurance*, "If you go to the doctor once a week, and take seven different medicines a week, you can do the math and see that it costs more than a car payment each month. That's not including if he needs a surgery, a chest X-ray, a CAT scan, or something else." All of these medical issues involve co-pays, deductibles, and other costs that add up over time.

During Zach's lengthy illnesses, Sharon's husband, Arnold,

MEDICAL BANKRUPTCIES ON THE RISE

by Elizabeth Warren, Professor, Harvard Law School, and Amelia Warren Tyagi, co-authors of *The Two-Income Trap: Why Middle Class Parents are Going Broke*

Having a child is now the single best predictor that a woman will go bankrupt. In fact, this year, more children will live through their parents' bankruptcy than their parents' divorce.

The causes for so much financial distress among parents are complex, but one fact stands out: Fully half of these families filed for bankruptcy in the wake of a medical problem.

The typical medical bankruptcy is solidly middle class. Most have been to college, gotten decent jobs, and bought homes. And they even bought health insurance—about three-quarters of medical bankruptcies had medical coverage when illness struck.

Medical bankruptcies look pretty much like other middle-class Americans, with one notable exception: They have children. A family with children is now about three times more likely to file for bankruptcy than their childless counterparts.

kept requesting more and more hours at work to keep up with the constant flow of medical bills. Arnold works for a heating and electrical company located in the Indiana area where they live, and as Sharon says, works as much as possible, "They usually cut him off somewhere between seventy and eighty hours per week." He was working hard to keep the family financially afloat, making about $65,000 per year. Sharon, a full-time mom, was busy at home caring for Zach and his two younger sisters, Dakota and Jessica.

Finally, about a year ago, Zach contracted a sinus infection that lasted from November through March, which left him on

Health insurance with holes wide enough to drive a bus through has caused some of the problem, as many families discover the real meaning of the fine print only after they have been denied coverage. Co-pays and uncovered services can also leave a family struggling with thousands of dollars in medical bills. And for the forty-three million Americans with no insurance, even a broken arm or an appendectomy can put a family in a deep financial hole.

Even when health insurance covers most of the doctor and pharmacy bills, families can find themselves caught in another financial nightmare—lost income. The majority of workers have no long-term disability insurance, which means that when a serious illness strikes and they are no longer able to work, they simply do without a paycheck. That might be tolerable for those families with ample savings, but today's middle class families essentially live paycheck to paycheck. Even if medical diagnosis is favorable, there may be little hope of financial recovery.

Every thirty seconds in the United States, someone files for bankruptcy in the aftermath of a serious health problem. Time is running out. A broken healthcare system is bankrupting families across this country.

antibiotics for five full months. Because insurance balked at covering more antibiotics, the doctor administered the medication through an IV line just to get around insurance restrictions. Sharon recalls, "The doctors were talking about flushing Zach's sinuses every time he had a sinus infection—and that involves surgery." More costly procedures were adding up, and Zach wasn't getting any better.

Sharon schedules Zach's visits to medical specialists all on the same day to save trips to the hospital. On the day they received the news that the sinus infection was still raging, they also had a visit with Zach's digestive specialist.

It had been a stressful day of CAT scans, IVs, and other procedures. By the time Zach and Sharon got to the digestive specialist's office Sharon was overwhelmed, "The doctor asked, 'How's everything going?' and I just lost it and started crying. I said, 'He's been sick for so long. I don't see how he can keep going like this forever.' The doctor responded, 'It's not my field, but it sounds like an immune problem to me.'

In the end, his digestive doctor is the one who figured out that Zach had an immune deficiency which caused him to get sick over and over again. The good news was that there was a treatment for this disease, once a month intravenous infusions of gamma globulin. The bad news was that after the insurance company paid what they cover, the medicine still costs $5,000 in of out-of-pocket expenses each year.

At this point, the family—fully insured, with Sharon's husband basically working the equivalent of two full-time jobs—was losing the battle of the medical bills. "When Zach was diagnosed with a primary immune deficiency, we knew it wasn't going to end," Sharon recalls. "We already had remortgaged our house to pay for medical bills—so when we found out how much the new treatment was going to cost, we knew we couldn't pay our higher mortgage payment, the cost of his medicines, and other costs every month." That was the breaking point.

Sharon and Arnold finally waved the white flag of surrender when it became clear that there simply weren't enough hours in the workweek to keep up with the constant incoming flow of bills. They made an appointment with an attorney to declare bankruptcy.

Their attorney's office was in downtown Indianapolis. After checking in with the receptionist, Sharon and Arnold were ushered to a large conference room that had two walls of windows, and another wall with shelves of law books from floor to ceiling. They settled down into comfortable chairs around a conference table and told the attorney their story, sharing all their raw feelings of despair that came from working hard, having a sick child, and still losing everything, "The attorney cried when we told him what had been happening with us. My husband really needed that because when we went there it was just breaking him. His theory was that he could just keep working more." But there weren't any more hours in the week left to work.

Medical issues are a leading cause of bankruptcy in the United States. A February 2005 study published in the journal *Health Affairs*, authored by a well-respected team of experts that includes several Harvard University professors, found that families like Sharon's are part of a growing trend of medical bankruptcies.[2] In fact, half of all bankruptcy filings in 2001 were related to medical issues.

And medical related bankruptcies are skyrocketing. There's been a twenty-threefold (2,300 percent) increase in medical related bankruptcy filings between 1981, when only 8 percent of bankruptcies were medical related, and 2001.[3] And, it turns out, these medical related bankruptcies look a lot like what Sharon's family experienced—most of those who went bankrupt had health insurance (a full 76 percent had insurance when their illness started),[4] and those filing for bankruptcy are "predominantly in the middle or working classes."[5] In other words, it's mostly hard-working families with insurance that end up in bankruptcy as they deal with medical issues.

"Our study is frightening. Unless you're Bill Gates, you're just one serious illness away from bankruptcy," notes Dr. David Himmelstein, the lead author of the study and an associate professor of medicine at Harvard in a Harvard Medical School Office of Public Affairs press release. "Most of the medically bankrupt were average Americans who happened to get sick. Health insurance offered little protection. Families with coverage faced unaffordable co-payments, deductibles, and bills for uncovered items like physical therapy, psychiatric care, and prescription drugs. And even the best job-based health insurance often vanished when prolonged illness caused job loss precisely when families needed it most. Too often, private health insurance is an umbrella that melts in the rain."[6]

After Sharon, Arnold, and Zach's story ran in the *New York Times* in October 2005,[7] the drug company dropped the $5,000 annual bill for uncompensated costs, and other help came their way. They are still in danger of losing their house, which is in foreclosure due to the bankruptcy, but the family is starting to save money again. Sharon concludes, "I'm going to seriously knock on wood. I can't imagine us being in the same situation now that our medical bills are covered."

Making it to the front page of the newspaper is not a viable solution for the other two million debtors and their dependents that experienced bankruptcies related to medical problems in 2001.[8] "Families with children were especially hard hit," notes the news release about the study put out by the Harvard Medical School Office of Public Affairs.[9] It continues, "—about 700,000 children lived in families that declared bankruptcy in the aftermath of serious medical problems." Something has to give.

The Melting Umbrella

The truth is that according to the World Health Organization, the United States spends more on healthcare per person than any other nation in the world,[10] yet still was only tied for the twenty-eighth highest life expectancy,[11] and ranked in at a low thirty-seventh for our mortality rate of children under five years old.[12] We aren't getting much for the money we spend.

Some states are trying to do something about this. For example, there's been a movement in California to get universal health coverage for kids, Maine is working on getting costs to businesses down while covering more people, and Vermont passed a bill that called for a publicly financed comprehensive healthcare system through the State House and State Senate in 2004 that was eventually vetoed by the Governor.

Dr. Deborah Richter, current Chair of Vermont healthcare For All, got tired of seeing her patients die from treatable diseases because they were uninsured and unable to pay for proper medical care. A few of her patients pushed her to activism: One situation involved a brother and sister who both had juvenile diabetes and didn't have insurance. They came from a hardworking family that made just enough money so they weren't eligible for Medicaid, but their jobs didn't come linked with health insurance. When their health worsened, they weren't able to take care of their health needs, leading to tragic consequences.

Like the siblings, many in our healthcare system are lost in the huge gaps in coverage, "Right now we have private insurance for most middle and upper income kids, and several low income coverage possibilities including Medicaid and SCHIP (State Children's Health Insurance Program), but we still have nine million kids falling through the cracks," notes Dr. Alison Buist, Health Policy Director for the Children's Defense Fund.

Some coverage is available to low-income families, Buist explains how it works. Medicaid, a federal entitlement program, requires the federal government to provide support if a person meets their eligibility criteria. It currently covers more than forty million people, half of whom are children.[13] SCHIP, a federal block grant program that provides funding to states, is essentially a state health insurance program that covers children from families with slightly higher incomes than Medicaid covers. Yet there are too many children and families who do not qualify for either program and are left without healthcare options.

Many of those are Americans who hold jobs without health insurance coverage. These workers make too much money to qualify for any state or federal medical assistance, yet the high cost of private insurance makes it out of reach, particularly for those holding low-income jobs (which are the jobs least likely to have job-linked health coverage). In fact, working families make up 81 percent of uninsured people.[14]

Patricia Schoeni, Executive Director of National Coalition on healthcare, notes, "Lots of people think that when you're talking about the uninsured, you're talking about poor people. But the majority of uninsured work; and a large number of them are middle class Americans. They are uninsured either because they work for an employer who doesn't provide health insurance and going out onto the open market to buy an individual insurance policy is prohibitively expensive; or they are uninsured because they are unemployed, or because employers are passing along the cost increases to them and they drop the coverage."

Not to give the wrong impression: People in poverty are also doing without healthcare in our nation. Right now, the Kaiser Family Foundation reports, "Low-income Americans with family incomes below 200 percent of the poverty level run the highest risk of being uninsured. Over a third of the poor and nearly 30 percent of the near-poor lack health insurance."[15] And again, these statistics are only those without health insurance, and don't include the significant number of Americans whose healthcare coverage would not carry them through a serious or long-term illness. Essentially, as Dr. Himmelstein, associate professor at Harvard, noted, unless you are Bill Gates and can pay unlimited sums out-of-pocket, you can't count on coverage in this country when the chips are down.

This crisis is only deepening, with the number of uninsured Americans rising quickly. Between 2000 and 2004 alone, the number of uninsured people under sixty-five years old increased by six million.[16] In that same time period, job-linked coverage dropped by 5 percent.[17]

The 5 percent drop in job-linked coverage is nothing to be glossed over. Frankly, the cost of employer-sponsored health insurance is going through the roof. Businesses are also struggling with the rising costs of healthcare. Many businesses are stretched to the limits of profitability just because of the escalating premiums for employees. There was an 11 percent increase in premium costs in the one year between 2003 and 2004. By 2004 the average cost of a premium for family coverage was $9,950.[18] The Kaiser Family Foundation finds, "Premiums for employer-sponsored health insurance rose at about five times the rate of inflation and workers earnings."[19] And it further notes, "Since 2000, premiums for family coverage have risen 59 percent."[20]

In this current situation of increasingly expensive healthcare coverage, the impacts are also seen in the way we work. Joan Williams, Professor of Law at the University of California,

Hastings, and Director of the Center for WorkLife Law, comments, "Healthcare is a huge reason why people overwork in the United States. One of the reasons people strive so hard to get 'good jobs' is because otherwise they wouldn't have health insurance. In the U.S. we tend to have bad twenty to twenty-five hour per week jobs without benefits, and good forty to sixty hour per week jobs with benefits. A lot of the reason people are willing to work such long hours is not that they prefer to do so, but because they have no other choice since we deliver healthcare through a job link.

"This has direct implications for moms," explains Williams, "because it pushes families into a format where one person has an all consuming job with healthcare, which means mothers get pushed into marginalized jobs or out of the labor force. Also, the lack of socially provided healthcare makes it very difficult for proportional pay and equity for part-time work because it's so expensive for an employer." She concludes, "Europe has a guarantee of part-time equity in their laws, and one of the reasons is healthcare. The lack of socially provided healthcare in the United States plays a major role in the fact that we work longer hours than virtually any industrialized country." These long hours, in turn, allow little time for raising a family.

The astronomical cost of healthcare coverage is not only changing the way we work, but has also caused a drop in job-linked healthcare coverage altogether. Many employers are simply unable to afford the sky-rocketing costs of health coverage for their employees, leading to an increasing number of uninsured Americans.

Uninsured Complications and the Ultimate Cost

There were forty-six million uninsured Americans in 2004.[21] Forty-six million Americans like Dr. Richter's patients, the uninsured siblings with juvenile diabetes who were unable to afford proper medication and treatment for a treatable condition. "I took care of them for years. When George was twenty-one-years-old, he essentially died from complications of diabetes. At the same time his sister, Tina, was five months pregnant and had a premature baby that didn't survive, mainly because the mother was a poor candidate for pregnancy after years of untreated diabetes. Then a year later, at twenty-five years old, Tina had a heart attack, ended up needing bypass surgery and died on the table. And this was just one family, but it became routine. These were people who didn't need to live this way."

Forty-six million Americans are like another of Dr. Richter's patients, a woman in her late fifties with post-menopausal bleeding. "She came to me because her family was begging her to see a doctor. She had obvious signs of cancer and I said, 'Look, here are the things we need to do.' And she said, 'I just can't afford it right now.' And she kept waiting. Then she had a pulmonary embolism and died, which is a sign of cancer. She just kept delaying and ignoring signs for at least a year and a half. She didn't do anything because she was afraid of the costs, but then she died." This woman paid the ultimate price with her life. People without insurance are right to fear high medical costs, but they shouldn't have to pay with their lives.

Ironically medical procedures and treatments often cost more for people who are *un*insured, than for people who are insured. A study prepared by the Hospital Accountability Project of the Service Employees International Union investigated this issue and found: "While insurance companies and other third-party payers have aggressively negotiated discounts for their health plan participants, the uninsured have been left behind. Without any bargaining power of their own, uninsured 'self-pay' hospital patients are expected to pay non-discount 'gross charges.' " The study further found, ". . . patients who pay full gross charges—typically the working poor who earn too much to qualify for Medicaid or charity care but are not covered by insurance—generally pay twice as much as the payment received for insured inpatients."[22] People without insurance, and those with inadequate private insurance, are on the front lines of our medical crisis.

Taking Action

After finishing her medical residency years ago, Dr. Richter worked in the inner city helping low income patients, but after six months she realized she could help more patients by working to reform health coverage in order to stop the medical crisis at the source. This decision came to her as she dealt with big issues, like the unnecessary deaths of her patients, and with the smaller issues, such as, "I would prescribe medicine. Then the patient would come back six months later and still not be better because they couldn't afford to fill their prescriptions."

So she started working part-time as a doctor and part-time as an advocate. Dr. Richter's resolve was strengthened as she compared her experiences with doctors in other countries. Once, when speaking in Canada where for more than three decades all citizens have been covered through a single-payer health plan (a system where the government pays the healthcare costs of citizens to independent, privately run hospitals, doctors, and other health services), she shared a story about how one of her uninsured patients died due to lack of care. "People in Canada asked, 'Did the newspapers cover it?'" Dr. Richter responded, "No, this was just one case of dozens and dozens I saw in my practice alone. Think about this magnified across our country."

As medical costs and the number of uninsured rise at an alarming rate, people are becoming ever more aware of America's healthcare crisis. "The current patchwork system we have isn't working," notes Buist. "We're trying to move toward a world in which children have access to all the advantages that we can easily give them if we just had good policy." Buist joins Dr. Richter and others who are educating policy makers and organizing communities around the country to demand the good health policies our children deserve. "The fight we're fighting now," says Buist, "is to make sure all children have healthcare coverage. How you get there is the question."

World Comparisons

The rest of the world is way ahead of us. "The United States remains the only Western nation without universal health insurance coverage," writes Rick Mayes in his book, *Universal Coverage: The Elusive Quest for National Health Insurance.* Two-thirds of the 191 countries tracked by the World Health Organization pay a higher percentage of their citizen's total healthcare costs than the U.S. does.[23]

Yet we, as a country, spend more on healthcare than any other nation in the world, a whopping $5,274 on average per capita,[24] and we don't have the best health outcomes, not even close. In fact, countries with the same mortality rate the United States has for children under five, spend a fraction of what the U.S. spends per person each year: Estonia ($263 per person); Slovakia ($265 per person); Poland ($303 per person); the UAE ($802 per person); and, the United States ($5,274).[25]

Our lack of complete healthcare coverage, coupled with these high costs has many shaking their heads in confusion. More money should equal more coverage and better care, right?

Not so. One big difference between the United States and other nations is that we are spending our health dollars mainly through prepaid private sector health insurance plans (In 2002, 65.7 percent of health expenditures came from private prepaid plans in the United States).[26] Few countries have such a high percentage of health expenditures through private prepaid plans. In fact, only seven other countries in the world had more than 50 percent of their health expenditures through private prepaid plans in 2002: the Bahamas, Chile, France, Nambia, the Netherlands, Slovenia, and South Africa.[27]

Private healthcare plans are notoriously inefficient with dollars, particularly since, more often than not, different prices are set for the same procedures and care based on what has been negotiated with various private health insurance coverage plans. The administrative effort it takes just to keep up with billing and accounting (since, for example, there can be a veritable multiple choice of prices for each medical procedure) adds significantly to the total healthcare cost. Not to mention the fact that it's quite difficult for a healthcare consumer to do "comparative shopping" when the prices aren't set.

This increased administrative spending through private insurers can be seen by comparing the administrative costs between public and private ventures right here in our own country: 12 percent of money spent by private insurers is spent on administrative efforts, while only 4 percent of money spent by Medicare (a public program) goes to administrative efforts.[28] Management salaries in private insurance firms have become more and more inflated, and profit may also have a hand in the difference. Many of the top CEOs from non-governmental, private health insurance companies are making tens of million dollars per year. For example, in 2004 the CEO of Aetna, Inc., a large health insurance company, brought home $10,119,290 in compensation including stock option grants. This particular CEO has another $164,722,382 in unexercised stock options.[29]

Canada offers a good example in how administrative costs differ between private and universal plans. Canada's national healthcare system offers universal health coverage paid by the government, as a single-payer; while the doctors, hospitals, and other medical service providers are still independent from the government (much as if our Medicare was expanded to cover our entire population). In 1999, on average, each person in the United States racked up $1,059 in administrative costs related to healthcare, while an average Canadian incurred $307 in administrative costs.[30] Australia, Denmark, Finland, Iceland, Sweden, and Taiwan have similar single-payer health plans.[31] It's important to note this coverage is not linked to a citizen's employer, as private coverage often is in the United States.

A 2004 study in the *International Journal of Health Sciences* found that such healthcare systems are significantly more efficient. "Our data help explain why Canadians spend 40 percent less on healthcare, yet receive more hospital care and make more doctor's visits and enjoy better access to care. Trimming U.S. administrative costs to Canadian levels would save at least $209 billion annually, enough to cover the uninsured and improve coverage for the tens of millions who are currently underinsured." The study also concludes that such reductions would be, ". . . enough to fund universal coverage."[32]

While many point to the Canadian single-payer system as a

template for solutions to our healthcare problems, there isn't a consensus as to what is the best healthcare solution for the United States at this time. To be perfectly clear, while we are advocating for universal coverage (particularly for children), we are not endorsing one healthcare solution, such as a single-payer system, over another. However, comparing Canada's healthcare system to our own is useful. Canada is a nation with a similar standard of living that enjoys a healthcare system that is serving its citizens more effectively by objective measures.

Dr. Reichter points out, "We can pick and choose features from around the world, it doesn't have to be Canada—we can pick the prevention and public health structure from Japan, or the primary care choices in England and Sweden. The thing

---

A COMPLEX DOWNFALL

by Dr. Bree Johnston, Associate Professor of Medicine, UC San Francisco; Co-President, California Physicians' Alliance

The U.S. spends about twice as much per person on healthcare as any other industrialized nation. Despite this, the U.S. is ranked thirty-seventh in terms of health system quality by the WHO, and many health indicators in the U.S.—infant mortality, life expectancy, and access to care—are worse in the U.S. than in other comparable nations. Forty six million Americans have no health insurance, and millions of others are underinsured. It is estimated that 18,000 adults die in the U.S. because of lack of health insurance. Half of bankruptcies are related to illness and medical bills. How can we spend so much and get so little?

One reason is that the U.S. operates the most logistically complex people have to recognize is that a universal healthcare system is inevitable. There is no other way out of the crisis than to have a universal healthcare system that includes everyone, contains costs, and is publicly financed." Clearly, when the time comes for change, there will be no lack of ideas for solutions.

The Will to Change

There is growing consensus that we have a problem. Then why, if there are so many possible solutions, are we stuck with this failing healthcare system? The answer: We have an entrenched and complex healthcare system that is hugely difficult to change. Historically, there has not been sufficient political capacity to create a plan and implement needed changes. Patricia Schoeni,

healthcare system in the world. We have over 7000 private health plans, and physicians and hospitals need an army of billing personnel to negotiate the complexity of their requirements. Studies have found that between 1 in 4 and 1 in 5 healthcare dollars are spent on administration. Many health plans are for-profit, and thus need to keep an eye on maximizing profits for their shareholders. So our system spends a lot of health dollars on elements that do not contribute to healthcare services at all.

Every other industrialized nation has some sort of universal health insurance coverage. The only thing that keeps the United States from doing the same is the powerful influence of the insurance and pharmaceutical industries, who are making out like bandits under the current system and would face huge financial losses under a new system. It will take a mass coalition to overcome these special interests. It is time to build that coalition.

Executive Director of National Coalition on Healthcare, agrees and points out, "There is no will to fix the problem right now. It is basically a lack of leadership in all levels of government and on Capitol Hill, and an unwillingness of elected representatives, the majority of them at least, to come to grips with the fact that we have a problem and we have to deal with it."

If individual tragedies like those shared by Dr. Richter don't provide impetus for change, maybe the business sector can. More and more business leaders are recognizing that the high cost of healthcare coverage is a major disadvantage that cuts into their ability to compete in a global market. Consequently, some business leaders are helping ignite the political will for addressing the healthcare issue with solid solutions. During the 2004 drive for comprehensive health coverage in Vermont, many businesses signed on to the effort and put signs in their windows that said, "This Business Supports Universal Healthcare." One such business, based out of Waitsfield, Vermont, is Small Dog Electronics. Small Dog Electronics, one of the larger Apple computer resellers in the United States, sells new, refurbished, and used Macintosh computer products, as well as other related products like iPods.

Each fall, beautiful crimson maple trees frame the entrance to the Small Dog offices and warehouse. Dogs are allowed at work, and every day about fifteen of them clock in with their owners. Don Mayer, CEO, brings his bulldog named Hammerhead and his pomeranian named Fantail Shrimp to work with him each day, "The dogs are a sort of reminder to keep my business small and friendly. That's why we named it Small Dog. I've been in business a long time and found that I always have less stress, more fun, and make more money when my business is small."

He comments, "We take our dogs very seriously, and we have every kind of dog you can imagine. We have some small dogs, we have mixed breeds, huskies, two black labs, a golden, a yellow lab, and eskies." There are dog bowls, toys, and dog beds throughout the offices and warehouse.

Small Dog Electronics, which prides itself in taking care of employees, currently covers all employees and their families with health insurance. This is beginning to be a problem. When Mayer started in business thirty years ago he notes, "The cost for a family healthcare premium was about $1,500 per year. Now it's approximately $11,000 for each family's coverage. This can amount to almost 50 percent of an entry level employee's salary." In fact, the cost of healthcare coverage is becoming a big factor in business decisions for Mayer, "No longer do I consider growth and opportunity as the criteria for expanding my staff. I have to consider the astronomical cost of healthcare as part of that equation as well. This makes the healthcare crisis an impediment to economic growth, which can be further illustrated by the number of labor actions and strife with healthcare as the primary element of dispute."

From his perspective, supporting comprehensive coverage "was a fairly easy decision for us," says Mayer. "The healthcare system as it's currently configured is a mishmash that basically represents an accident of history." Sharing his understanding, Mayer continues, "This employer based healthcare system is completely faulty. It was instituted in the 1940s as a way to get around the wage price controls from WWII and after so employers could offer health insurance as an incentive to retain key employees. It kind of stuck over the years to the point where we are now, which is a healthcare system on the verge of collapse."

It's not just small businesses that are starting to take serious notice of the implications of our healthcare system. In 2005, Toyota announced it is planning to build a second plant in Ontario that will hire about 1,300 workers and make 100,000 cars each year starting in 2008. The Canadian location was chosen over cities in the United States despite the fact that several U.S. states offered "hundreds of millions of dollars in subsidies," as reported by CBC News.[33] The CBC News article noted, "In addition to lower training costs, Canadian workers are also $4 to $5 cheaper to employ partly thanks to the taxpayer-funded health-care system in Canada, said federal Industry Minister David Emmerson. 'Most people don't think of our health-care system as being a competitive advantage,' he said." Some executives of big businesses, particularly those from the vehicle manufacturing industry like General Motors, Ford, and in particular DaimlerChrysler, are starting to bring up the fact that another type of healthcare system might be better for business.[34]

There still isn't a full-fledged push for change from corporate America at this time. This boils down, in part, to a philosophical issue since many in big businesses are opposed to increased federal government involvement as a rule, and addressing comprehensive health coverage certainly entails more federal government involvement. However, as American healthcare costs continue to streak upward at an incredible pace, there's no question that leaving our healthcare linked to employers is going to hurt our competitive advantage in a global economy. Our economy, our businesses, and our citizens are struggling. It's long past time for a change.

The Big Picture

Our healthcare system is in crisis. Year after year the cost of healthcare rises at a multiple of the inflation rate. Every year fewer businesses provide healthcare for employees. Every year the number of Americans who have healthcare coverage has declined. Because of this, more and more people find themselves without health insurance, without access to preventative care, and without access to any healthcare at all save the emergency room.

These emergency rooms visits are often for illnesses that need never have become so severe, and for illnesses that would regularly be treated by a primary care physician much less expensively. This also puts added pressure on the ability of emergency rooms to properly care for patients, not only because they end up being a place of last resort for those without funds to pay for services (and often end up stuck with the bill), but also because the added numbers of those without insurance or other healthcare options often fill emergency rooms to capacity, making them unavailable for other critical emergency services.

It has become conventional wisdom that patients in emergency rooms and hospitals need a relative or friend that can stay with them in order to advocate on their behalf as they negotiate chaotically overcrowded emergency rooms and understaffed hospitals. "Hundreds of thousands of people die each year from medical errors, and millions are injured by poor quality care and accidents that shouldn't be happening," says Patricia Schoeni, Executive Director of National Coalition on healthcare. Schoeni notes that the three main drivers in our current healthcare crisis are cost, coverage, and quality of care—and that all must be addressed as we form healthcare solutions.

We don't need to read statistics about how poorly our medical system compares to other industrialized countries. It's a reality we all understand. "We do more research than any other country, the problem is we don't have the ability or facilities to put what we know how to do best into actual practice on a broad scale," Schoeni explains. In other words, while we have some of the best healthcare technology in the world, very few people get access to those services.

The crisis of our medical system not only brings the loss of a secure medical safety net for American citizens, the cost of this failing system is also undermining our economy. As car manufacturers and other large companies make decisions about where to locate their manufacturing centers, the U.S. will continue to lose when competing with lower associated healthcare costs.

Businesses in the U.S. are fundamentally at a competitive disadvantage in the global economy because of the cost of healthcare.

Our economy is suffering in yet another respect due to the exorbitant cost of healthcare. The fact that medical costs have become a primary cause of bankruptcy is really only the canary in the coal mine. American families have less disposable income and more debt due to the skyrocketing costs of medical care. This depresses the overall economy just like high oil prices do when the high cost of gasoline eats up a family's budget.

The costs of medical benefits are also distorting the way businesses structure the workplace. Why do you think businesses are willing to pay overtime rather than hire additional workers, even though overworked employees are more likely to make mistakes and be less productive? The costs of benefits have become so burdensome that many employers bend over backwards to avoid hiring additional full-time workers. Some employers "specialize" in hiring part-time workers to avoid paying benefits altogether. One consequence of this trend is that a substantial portion of the working poor have two or three part-time jobs, none with benefits. These hardworking people are just an illness away from financial ruin. Many employers are also having financial difficulty with high premiums and are passing along the increased costs to their employees, making healthcare benefits one of the main issues of contention when unions strike. The fact is that employers and employees are both experiencing huge difficulty due to our healthcare crisis. This situation has to change.

Steps for Change

There are certain steps that must be taken to address this crisis. To start, all children in the United States must have health coverage. As terrible as the lack of healthcare coverage is for adults, it's unconscionable not to protect our children, and it is extremely short-sighted to leave children without medical coverage. Plainly said, providing easily accessed healthcare to children will save us medical costs in the short and long term. It will also enable those children to learn and grow into the citizens that are going to be supporting us as we retire in the future. As Buist points out, "Covering kids is not just about health. Getting children access to healthcare has ramifications in almost every area of their lives, and the lives of their families."

The *Motherhood Manifesto* promotes basic, highly interrelated steps to better support parents and children. Healthcare is a core part of this support. The fact of the matter is that mother-friendly work would be more available if we had some kind of universal healthcare. Our childcare providers would be better able to stay working at the jobs they love if they had healthcare. Minimum wage workers would not be quite so vulnerable if they had healthcare. Finally, every child's parent also needs access to healthcare. As the flight attendants always reminds us right before an airplane takes off, "In the event of a loss of pressure, place the oxygen mask securely over your own face before assisting your child." Point being, it is hard to take care of our children if we are incapacitated.

Why do we first call for universal healthcare for all children, and not for all Americans? Restructuring our healthcare system is a monumental task. There will be major conflicting powers involved in creating this change, and so far all efforts have stalled out. Taking care of kids is something we must do today. We should work with whatever systems we have to give all children access to healthcare immediately. Then hopefully we can celebrate the transition to universal healthcare for all citizens in the not so distant future.

Keeping our children healthy and protecting them from injury or illness should never be left to chance; healthcare for children should not be a privilege in America but a right. Simply put, the time has come for all children to have access to healthcare.

Chapter "H"—Healthcare for All Kids

More and more families and children in our country have inadequate healthcare coverage and forty-six million Americans are completely uninsured. As a result far too many families are either foregoing needed care or ending up in bankruptcy. Many mothers find themselves nursing a gravely ill child and facing financial ruin, all at the same time. This should never happen in America.

ACTION: While our leaders come to grips with the healthcare emergency facing the nation, mothers want—

(1) Congress to immediately enact universal coverage for all American children.

International Health Care Comparisons

- The United States spends more on healthcare per person than any other nation in the world. [i]

- Was tied for the 28th highest life expectancy. [ii]

- Ranked a low 37th for our mortality rate of children under five years old. [iii]

- Two-thirds of the 191 countries tracked by the World Health Organization pay a higher percentage of their citizen's total health care costs than the U.S. does. [iv]

- As a country, United States citizens spend more on health care than any other nation in the world, a whopping $5,274 on average per capita. [v]

- Countries with the same mortality rate as the United States has for children under five, spend a fraction of what U.S. citizens spend per person each year: Estonia ($263 per person); Slovakia ($265 per person); Poland ($303 per person); the UAE ($802 per person); and, the United States ($5,274). [vi]

i. http://www.who.int/whr/2005/annex/annexe6_en.pdf

ii. http://www.who.int/whr/2005/annex/annexe1_en.pdf

iii. http://www.who.int/whr/2005/annex/annexe2a_en.pdf

iv. http://www.who.int/whr/2005/annex/annexe5_en.pdf

v. http://www.who.int/whr/2005/annex/annexe6_en.pdf, www.who.int/whr/2005/annex/annexe2a_en.pdf

vi. www.who.int/whr/2005/annex/annexe2a_en.pdf, http://www.who.int/whr/2005/annex/annexe6_en.pdf

To support change, go to **www.MotherhoodManifesto.com.**

6

Excellent Childcare

Trading her princess nightgown for jeans and a blue denim jacket, Haylee had her binky clipped to her shirt and her hair pulled up into pigtails with bows. She stepped out of her bedroom that her mom, Kim, had decorated for her in lavender and aqua, ready for her big day. The sun was just starting to peek through her curtains making pools of light on the cozy butterfly quilt on her bed.

It was Haylee's first day at a childcare center, and Kim's first day at a new job.

They got in the car and drove down a tree-lined hill, took a left at the stoplight, and then pulled into the daycare about a mile down the street. Kim had looked long and hard for quality care for Haylee that was also affordable and close to home.

Several weeks earlier, after hours of research and touring several childcare facilities—some clearly substandard (one with a frazzled teacher crying into a phone in the corner), some full with long waiting lists, and some with very young teachers surrounded by absolute chaos in their classrooms—Kim saw that many of the childcare workers simply weren't given the resources they needed to succeed in their classrooms, and that lack of resources came through loud and clear as she toured.

Kim finally chose the center where she was now dropping off Haylee. The center was one of the more expensive and "prestigious" childcare facilities in the area, and although Kim still had some questions about that program, her job was starting, and it was the only real option. There simply weren't many high-quality daycares in Kim's community.

With her childcare search, Kim joined the more than 30 percent of parents who (according to a 2000 survey commissioned by the I Am Your Child Foundation and *Parents* magazine) say finding affordable quality childcare is difficult.[1] This lack of accessibility is a key issue, particularly as millions of children need care every day while their parents work. In fact, the Children's Defense Fund estimates that each day twelve million children under five years old spend time being cared for by someone other than a parent[2] —this is nearly two-thirds of all children in that age group.[3] While this book explores ways to give parents more time with their families through policies like flexible work options and paid family leave, there will always be a need for quality childcare so that parents can work and support their families.

The first day Kim left Haylee, both of them cried. Kim held her tears until the parking lot while Haylee cried hysterically in the classroom. Kim expected that she'd have to deal with some initial separation anxiety, as is the norm with many small children. What she didn't expect was the callous response from Haylee's teacher.

HIGH COST OF CARE

A Children's Defense Fund study found childcare in the United States costs between $4,000 and $10,000 a year for each child, with the costs rising for babies and younger children, special-needs kids, and kids living in parts of the country where the cost of living is higher.[33]

To put this cost in perspective, consider that a full one-quarter of families with children under age six earned less than $25,000 in 2001.

Haylee's main teacher had seemed nice at first, a bit stern perhaps, but nothing stood out as a problem. The morning Kim's impression of the teacher changed is fixed in her memory: "She started getting borderline mean to the kids, behaving in a way that was odd considering she was working with two- and three-year-old children." One day when Kim came to pick up Haylee, she first stopped outside the door to look through a window into the classroom and saw Haylee crying. She then heard the teacher say, "Stop crying and acting like a baby." The teacher proceeded to swat Haylee's binky out of her mouth, saying, "You're not a baby. You don't need a binky, and you should stop crying." Haylee was two years old.

Kim went to the management and asked to have Haylee transferred out of that teacher's classroom, which they did. She recalls, "I was miserable and angry with the childcare center, and I was also disappointed in myself for allowing it to happen to my child for the short period of time that it did." Haylee clearly wasn't happy in the situation, and Kim felt trapped because she needed to work and there weren't other obvious childcare options.

Haylee finished out the year doing well in her new classroom. When she moved up a year and started in her third classroom, it became clear to Kim that the high staff turnover was a big problem. It was like a revolving door. By Kim's count, in Haylee's series of three classrooms, she had twelve different teachers and assistants. Sadly, Kim was discovering a reality of childcare in this country—that of high staff turnover due to low pay, lack of healthcare benefits, and minimal support for the providers. One study of childcare centers in California found that between 1996 and 2000 there was a 76 percent staff turnover rate.[4] This issue, combined with the fact that the United States has one of the higher students to teacher ratios in the world (the U.S. tied for ninety-first of 151 countries in preprimary student-to-staff ratios[5]), is a recipe for poor quality care.

The teacher transitions were hard on the kids in Haylee's class. Kim recalls, "The kids would get used to a teacher, but then they'd quit and the kids would have to start all over again.

And this was in a prestigious preschool which was about $900 per month!" Not only was the teacher turnover and lack of training taking a toll, the cost of even that quality of care was hard to afford for Kim. "The price of that childcare took all of my paycheck, and my parents had to step in to help support us."

In fact, quality childcare without some type of subsidy is unaffordable for many American families. Consider that a full one-quarter of families with children under age six earned less than $25,000 in 2001.[6] Add that to the fact that only one out of seven kids that are federally eligible for childcare assistance actually gets any help.[7] This is a failing system.

In fact, America ranks low in global comparisons of childcare support: The United States ranks twentieth out of seventy-two countries in terms of the percentage of Gross Domestic Product (GDP) spent on early childhood education.[8] A report by the Project on Global Working Families out of Harvard University concludes, "Initial inequities across social class are markedly exacerbated by the public policy decisions the United States has made, including, among others, the failure thus far to provide public preschool or early childhood education to parallel public school. . . . In many other nations, working families can count on publicly guaranteed parental leave; and in many, preschool childcare or early-childhood education is already publicly provided."[9]

This is a missed opportunity for our country. Excellent childcare has been proven again and again to have longstanding economic and educational benefits. The National Institute of Child

Health and Human Development, as reported by the Children's Defense Fund, found, "Children in higher quality care for their first four-and-a-half years of life scored higher on tests of cognitive skills, language ability, vocabulary, and short-term memory and attention than children in lower quality care."[10] One study (*Significant Benefits* by Lawrence Schweinhart and others) that researched the long-term impacts of good quality childcare for low-income children came to a similar conclusion, the Children's Defense Fund reports. That study found, "After 27 years, each $1 invested saved over $7 by increasing the likelihood that children would be literate, employed, and enrolled in postsecondary education, and making them less likely to be school dropouts, dependent on welfare, or arrested for criminal activity or delinquency."[11] Early learning opportunities will help build a generation of responsible, smart, and working adults. Yet these opportunities aren't widely available in America.

Yasmine Daniel, of the Children's Defense Fund, is concerned. "We feel childcare should be accessible and affordable to every family, and clearly it's not when right now childcare costs families between $4,000 and $10,000 per year." She suggests we think of early childhood education as we think of other education, noting, "When a young adult goes to college we subsidize their education. Ironically, at that point, parents are usually further along in their careers and are often more able to afford the costs of education than when their children are younger and they are just at the beginning of their earning potential. Generally, we are for subsidizing childcare on a sliding scale based on parental income."

Back at the childcare center, Haylee's problems were escalating. Although the teachers were nice to the students in her third classroom, they just weren't very organized or engaged in what was going on with the kids. "Sometimes I'd go there and the teacher wouldn't even be in the classroom. They'd be in another room, or on the phone a lot," notes Kim. And Haylee, then four years old, was getting picked on regularly by three other boys in her class. "I told the teachers several times about what was happening to Haylee in her classroom, but nothing changed and the teacher was completely out of it. And then I went to pick up Haylee one day and found out a little boy had kicked her hard in the stomach."

"That was it for me. The kick in the stomach pushed me over the edge. I took Haylee out and she never went back there," remembers Kim. At that point Kim's mom was able to cut back at work and watch Haylee for the next five months. The next year Haylee went to school in a Montessori preschool program, which she loved.

Kim felt enormous relief when she finally found good childcare for Haylee, "There weren't any screaming kids running around. On my first site visit, I was there for an hour and a half and everything was so under control—the children were smiling, happy, and learning. I wanted to break down and start crying because I felt like such a mean parent for sticking my child in

CHILDCARE IN AMERICA

Of preschool children in childcare arrangements because their mothers work, 10 percent are cared for by "nannies, babysitters in their homes, or other similar non-relative situations"; 11 percent are in the care of independent, in-home daycare providers; 31 percent are in childcare centers or preschools; and 48 percent are in the care of relatives.[36]

that horrible daycare for two years." Unfortunately, this Montessori preschool wasn't initially available for Haylee because at first she was too young to attend, and then she was waitlisted before being admitted. The Montessori preschool was also quite expensive.

Clearly the quality of care at the first childcare center Haylee attended was substandard; the teachers didn't have appropriate training, the pay wasn't high enough to retain good teachers, and the classroom regularly bordered on chaos. Haylee's experience in the childcare center is particularly troubling because it occurred in a center that was supposedly one of the best in the area. All too often childcare facilities have uneven, poor quality care. The Children's Defense Fund reports that a study (*Cost, Quality, and Child Outcomes in Childcare Centers*) examining childcare in four states found, "childcare at most centers in the United States is poor to mediocre," with 12 percent of centers providing less than minimal quality care—defined as care that could harm "children's health, safety, and development." As for the centers that rated well for good quality care, those comprised only 14 percent.[12]

There are a wide variety of childcare configurations, ranging from childcare centers and preschools, to in-home care by independent providers, and informal care by relatives and friends. Though this variety of options sounds comprehensive, they are not numerous enough to provide for all the children who need care. With increasing frequency, grandparents or other relatives, who sometimes fill childcare gaps, are having to work into their later years to support themselves, making them less available for childcare assistance. Families are stretched thin. In fact, due to high costs and otherwise inaccessible programs, many school-age children end up home alone or caring for younger siblings before they are ready to handle that responsibility.

Too few American families have access to excellent childcare, and the poor-quality care many are receiving can harm children in the short-term and effect long-lasting damage: A recent study found that inadequate childcare situations negatively impact future educational achievements, with kids in lower quality childcare scoring lower on cognitive-ability tests.[13] A growing number of families have two parents in the labor force, making excellent childcare a necessity, not a luxury.

Childcare Providers Also Caught in Bind

It's not just families that are caught in the childcare bind of high costs, quality issues, and low availability. Childcare providers also struggle, particularly with low wages.

The average childcare provider earns a salary of just $18,060 a year.[14] Low salaries in turn lead to high turnover rates because of the financial hurdles faced by the childcare providers, many of whom are parents themselves. In fact, what

LOW SALARIES FOR CHILDCARE PROVIDERS

Childcare providers earn a salary of just $18,060 a year on average.[34]

can happen, particularly with childcare providers that care for children in their own homes, is that providers actually end up *subsidizing* the families whose children they watch. They end up paying out-of-pocket for food and educational supplies, but are unable to charge higher rates to parents for their time because many parents simply cannot afford to pay any higher rates.

Angenita is an in-home independent childcare provider in Illinois whose clients mainly come from a state-subsidized program.

In tears, Angenita had to tell her childcare assistant that she was going to delay paying her yet again because the state was behind on their payments for the children. She was embarrassed and horrified that she couldn't pay her assistant for work that was already done, but she, herself, hadn't been paid by the state in six months. The state program was supposed to work like clockwork: In-home childcare providers watched children that qualified for state subsidies, and the state paid the childcare providers those subsidies. In this case, the clock was broken.

Yet she kept her center open because "at that point I was dedicated to the field. I'd been in childcare for six months and didn't have another job avenue immediately available. I was stuck. I already quit my other job. I also had parents relying on me everyday. I couldn't just wake up and say, 'Okay it's all over. Find someone else to take care of the children.' "

She notes that with eight children in her care, if she stopped providing childcare then eight sets of parents would be forced to take time off work to find another sitter. And she knew these families well, knew they desperately needed her services in order to go to work to support their families—she was watching her sister's children, and also children on her block. Another factor, Angenita's a fighter: "I'm not one to accept failure. I had to think positively like, 'Okay, the check is coming soon.' I never imagined it would take that long." While childcare providers are often woefully underpaid, this situation was over the top.

Angenita's doorbell rang less than an hour after the tearful discussion. It was a union organizer named Maggie. Maggie sat down with Angenita and asked if she had any issues that need to be addressed with late checks from the state or other topics. "I said, 'Late checks! I've never even gotten mine,' and then I just started talking and talking," she recalls. Maggie told Angenita that there are a lot of providers in the same situation, and that there are even providers who lost their homes because of the state's failure to pay in a timely manner. Then she invited Angenita to an in-home childcare providers' union organizing meeting, and asked her to speak.

Several days later Angenita went to that meeting. She stepped out the front door of her house and drove to the center of Chicago's downtown. It was 1996. As she parked her car and entered a building with an old bicycle shop on the ground floor, she anticipated finally getting a chance to connect with other childcare providers in situations similar to hers.

Ready to take action, Angenita walked purposefully through the lobby to the elevator waiting area. The elevator door opened, Angenita pressed floor four, and her ride up began. Stepping out of the elevator, she turned and walked through an open door into a small conference room packed with at least forty women.

Angenita got up to speak about her role as a childcare provider and people listened. "I talked about the fact that I'm a teacher, a cook, a lawyer, a doctor, a nurse, a psychologist, a psychiatrist, a mediator, a cleaner, a mind reader, and an employer as well as an employee, and I have not been paid for the services that I do render."

The ice was broken. Women broke into applause, and cheers were called out after every title Angenita named. "Everyone was yelling. Im a cook (Yeah!)! I'm a mind reader (Yeah!)! Yeah!!!"

Her speech continued. "There is a difference between a need and a want, and just like oxygen to breathe, we need a living wage to live. With all the many hats I wear daily the state only wants to pay me $2.53 an hour per child and I have not been paid yet for six months."

The crowded room was awash with clapping and cheering.

The women who filled the room were also in-home childcare providers for the Illinois state childcare subsidy program in which the state allocates funds to providers based on a sliding scale of parent earnings. The state was behind in payments, not just for Angenita, who had been watching eight children a day for six months without pay, but for many other providers as well. On the day of the union meeting, Angenita was excited to share her predicament and experiences with other childcare providers and find out how to make a positive difference for everyone.

The organizing was a success. After banding together with the help of the Service Employees International Union (SEIU) and lobbying the Illinois state legislature, the childcare providers began to see real change.

"In 1999 we got a living wage increase from $19.18 to $20.50 per child *per day* from the state. In 2000 we got another increase for the cost of living, and in 2004 the federal subsidized food program increased payments for the children's food," notes Angenita.

In 2005 the SEIU had an election, the biggest in Illinois history and second biggest nationally, and 49,000 providers voted to officially unionize, becoming the first union of state-subsidized home childcare providers in the nation. These women and men are making history and positive changes for families right this very moment. As Angenita says, "We're a powerful force when you think about it. We're the people who take care of children after they enter the world."

Angenita is not alone. Tens of thousands of family childcare providers in more than twelve states around the country are organizing through unions. For example, SEIU and the American Federation of State, County and Municipal Employees

(AFSCME) are working together to organize over 45,000 family childcare providers in California. In Oregon 5,000 family child-care providers won the right to a union with AFSCME in 2005. They are now headed to the bargaining table to fight for health insurance and other benefits that childcare providers need.

Higher wages, benefits, and better public funding help both childcare workers and children. Low salaries and poor benefits lead to high provider turnover rates, creating unstable situations for our nation's children. Increased wages, as well as funding for continuing education for childcare providers, are needed to attract, and retain, top quality providers. And the benefit of top quality providers is incalculable: "Millions of preschoolers are spending precious years caught in a maze of unstable, substan-dard settings that compromise their chances of succeeding in school. For them, the years of promise represent lost opportunity at a crucially formative stage in their development," states a Carnegie Corporation report.[15]

Parents Also Caught in Economic Crunch

Long-term solutions are needed just as urgently on the parent side of the childcare equation. After all, it's not just the childcare providers like Angenita who are dealing with an inadequate, broken system. Even with the low salaries childcare providers receive, childcare itself is often too expensive for many working families. A Children's Defense Fund study found childcare in the United States costs between $4,000 and $10,000 a year for each child, with the costs rising for babies and younger children, special-needs kids, and kids living in parts of the country where the cost of living is higher.[16]

Ten thousand dollars per year, per child, is simply out of reach for many families. The big picture shows a tremendous number of American families in crisis. Remember, a full one-quarter of families with children under age six earned less than $25,000 in 2001.[17] Consequently, many families have only informal and sometimes dangerous, or inadequate childcare options because they are free or affordable. All too often the TV becomes the primary sitter, not to forget latchkey children that are too young to really take care of themselves. Parents are simply left with too few affordable, accessible, quality childcare options.

> **MOTHERS ARE IMPOR-TANT BREADWINNERS: CHILDCARE IS A NEED, NOT A LUXURY**
>
> A 1995 study, *Women: The New Providers,* interviewed women and found 55 percent brought in half or more of their household income (18 percent brought in all of the income, 11 percent more than half, and 26 percent brought in half). And of those in married families, 48 percent of working women brought in half or more of the household income.[37]

These three criteria—accessibility, affordability, and quality—define precisely what parents need. Accessibility means that parents are able to find and get their children into good childcare programs, not simply onto a long waiting list. Affordability indicates childcare costs that also allow parents to pay other necessary monthly expenses, like food and rent.

Defining high-quality childcare is more complicated, and requires a number of factors to come together: The providers need to be well-trained, supported, and paid a living wage; the facilities need to be safe; educational materials need to be up to date; healthy food needs to be available; there should be low provider turnover; and more. In order to assure quality childcare, some have suggested implementing uniform quality standards that govern all childcare and early education programs across the nation. Other possibilities include requiring state licensing and provider education, as well as seeking ways to increase the salaries necessary to attract and keep good childcare providers.

How do we handle this crisis, where providers are paid too little and the cost to parents is still prohibitively high? Childcare centers generally aren't making high profits either. Frankly, childcare doesn't come with a low price tag. Fixing this system requires a real investment by the community, much as we support the public school system. Decades ago, because more mothers were home with their children, childcare wasn't a necessity for as many families. Today, with most parents working, good childcare is essential. As a country it is time to ask: Why do we support an eight year old with public school funding and not a four year old?

Military Dreams

Surprisingly, there is a successful model childcare system operating right here in our country, and it might not be where you expect: the military. At this very moment, the Department of Defense has over 200,000 children in their care.[18] Two hundred thousand children. It's such a good system that many tout it as *the* example of large scale success—among those is the National Women's Law Center Co-President Nancy Duff Campbell, who in 2005 said, "The military's systemic approach to childcare continues to serve as a model for our nation's civilian childcare needs."[19]

Many of the problems outlined in this chapter have been successfully dealt with in the military childcare system. For example, care is available on a sliding scale to parents to make it affordable. Parents have easy access to the military childcare system and don't end up lost on long waiting lists. The military offers high-quality care, fair compensation and training for providers, and holds its centers to national uniform standards. Of the nearly holy trinity of childcare needs—affordability, quality, and accessibility—the military hits the mark with all three.

One person taking advantage of the military childcare system is Wendy. Wendy married her high school sweetheart after they first met at a county fair in Idaho; she was only sixteen when they first met. She and her girlfriends were walking into the fair, and he was leaving for the night. As they passed each other on the grass path lined with noisy fair games—toss the ring around the bowling pins, shoot the ducks, dart the balloons—and with the happy screams of roller coaster riders in the background, they recognized each other from their high school hallways.

She remembers the sticky sweet smell of cotton candy that night. It was summer. Wendy was sixteen when their eyes met and the, "Oh hi," passed her lips to her future spouse.

Then they started talking, and got along so well that he

borrowed a magic marker and wrote his phone number directly on her arm. She called him the next day before the marker could wash off, and they talked for hours. They talked through high school, taking a break to dance at her senior prom, and right into marriage when she was eighteen.

Just after she got married, Wendy had a baby, and her husband joined the military. Now twenty-four, Wendy and her husband have two children, Naomi is five and Xavier is just over one year. The childcare services provided by the military have been essential. When asked where her family would be without it, Wendy answers, "Poor. We would have struggled a lot more than we are now. We're better off mostly because of the subsidized childcare offered by the military."

Wendy's financial assessment is accurate. The cost difference of subsidized military childcare really makes a difference. Consider that in the Army a family that makes below $28,000 annually pays no more than $43 per week for childcare, or around $2,000 annually.[20] And then compare that to the national average cost of childcare, which can rise to $10,000 per year or more.[21] Childcare subsidies make a real difference, particularly as the number of children and families who live in poverty grows. According to the U.S. Census, 35.9 million Americans lived in poverty in 2003, up from 31.6 million just three years before.[22]

Wendy's children aren't the only members of her family who benefit from the higher standard of military childcare. Wendy also works at the facility, where her pay is significantly higher than if she worked at a nonmilitary daycare. Full-time pay at civilian childcare facilities averages out to $8.47 per hour, compared to military entry-level wages of between $9.34 and $13.23 per hour.[23] The military pay can go up to $18 per hour for classroom leads with Child Development Associate degrees.[24] In fact, the Department of Defense has taken the added step of creating policies to ensure caregivers are paid similar wages to those who work for the Department of Defense in other jobs that require similar amounts of "training, experience, and seniority."[25]

In the end, it's actually the very affordability of military childcare that allows Wendy to work at all. Without the subsidized childcare, Wendy would run the risk of making less money than the family pays out for childcare—a catch-22 that afflicts many modern families. "I wouldn't be going to work without the subsidy here," Wendy recognizes, "and we definitely would be having more financial problems if I wasn't going to work."

While some may picture military childcare as harsh classrooms full of kids in uniform with strict, noncreative curriculum, that's far from the truth. Many parents find their children are warmly welcomed and that their children respond in turn. Alberta, mother of two, has a daughter in a military childcare facility. Daliyah is four years old and full of life. She's learning fast, including learning to speak Spanish right along with English, and runs into her classroom each morning to greet her teachers with a warm, snug hug. Each night Daliyah includes her teachers in her bedtime prayers of good wishes.

The attention to provider training and curriculum detail shows when you enter a military childcare center. The Clarkmore Development Center at Ft. Lewis in Washington, for example, has a ratio of ten children to one teacher, and serves infants through school-age children. Each classroom has several age-appropriate learning stations. These learning stations range from art areas, sensory tables, play stages, music and "gross motor" or big movement rooms, to book listening stations, reading and writing centers, and all sorts of other learning activities that the teachers and students fit into their regular daily curriculum. The sound of happy kids playing floats in from the outside play area, yet chaos is kept to a creative minimum. The space is designed for child safety with windows into all closets, open restrooms, and open-view corridors through the classrooms.

Art, ideas, and colorful sponge paintings decorate the classroom walls, pictures of kids and teachers hang outside the classroom doors, and the smell of hot food fills the air at lunchtime. One such wall lists preschoolers' ideas for the definition of "dissect": "Sounds like an insect to me." "Dissect is a glove." "You have to cut before you eat." "It sounds like a broken fish." These young children were working on water curriculum and

HIGH QUALITY CARE SAVES MONEY IN THE LONG TERM

Studies show that investments in quality early education for preschoolers saves money in the long run through a reduction in crime rates and welfare needs, and also by lowering the need for special education and grade repeating. High-quality early education is an investment that pays off in the future.[35]

learning about fish (including how sometimes people dissect fish). They also worked with a water table and water animals—a favorite being the pretend turtles—and listened to curriculum-related stories. There was clearly enthusiastic, controlled learning going on in those classrooms.

These creative sparks don't happen by accident. The military has a rigorous childcare provider-training program designed to raise staff quality and pay, as well as uniform certification standards with an enforcement component based on regular inspections.[26] The military also has a uniform accreditation system, which has built in ways to assist providers in giving better care and education.[27] The Army, for example, requires extensive initial training for eighteen months, with an ongoing annual training requirement of twenty-four hours per year.[28] A childcare provider's employment is dependent on training, and all go through national and local background clearance checks.

Although the federal government is a long way from implementing an adequate nationally subsidized childcare program despite a host of proven benefits, there are local programs scattered across the country. A Wisconsin study that looked at the impacts of extending their kindergarten through twelfth grade education system to include free preschool for four-year-olds found that such programs save money in the long run. The study found early education reduces later crime rates and welfare needs, while increasing the total educational cost-benefit by 68 percent—partly through lowering the need for special education (saving $42 million) and students needing to repeat grades less often.[29]

Helen Blank, a nationally recognized leader in childcare policy from the National Women's Law Center, shares her dream vision for the future of childcare in America. "My ideal solution would be to have universal childcare—first it would start with paid family leave so parents have the choice of staying home those first few months, and then ideally at least some of the childcare would be available on a sliding scale, and some would be universally available for no cost." Blank envisions a future where some parts of childcare are universally funded just like the public K–12 school system.

Blank's ideal fix for now? "I'd give childcare programs money through the federal childcare Development Block Grant so we could have a combination of neighborhood childcare centers that are networked around a core resource referral program that could offer training, support, materials, and more—the military has a similar structure." Support like that envisioned by Blank is needed more now than ever. Federal funding for childcare has been frozen for four years, laments Blank, while at the same time the number of people in poverty—the very people who most need help with childcare costs—has grown. In fact, in the face of budget trouble, many states have been cutting their childcare assistance programs. The lack of public funding for childcare further impacts the accessibility, quality, and affordability of good care. In addition, new welfare-to-work requirements that went into place in the 1990s increased the number of parents in the workplace while the childcare supply remained relatively stagnant.[30] Sad to say, childcare in low-income communities is the least available.[31]

Other Options

Lettecia was breaking up with her boyfriend, and with two children between them she was worried about staying afloat as a single mom. Her son Alex was about a year old, and her son Mason was two. Lettecia was worried about paying for childcare, working, and also going back to school so she could change to a more lucrative career. She clearly remembers the moment she found out about a nonprofit subsidized childcare center available in her town.

She was working in an H & R Block office with the standard green accent walls and crisp setting. It was a rainy winter day; there was just enough of a chill in the air to combine with the rain in a way that sent the cold under doors, through windowpanes, and directly to the bones. The office was slow that day because it was the beginning of January and people weren't rushing in to file their taxes.

One woman did walk through the door that day, though. It was a client with an unscheduled appointment, and Lettecia walked up and introduced herself. Then they both went back to Lettecia's desk to look at the client's tax documents, "She pulled out her tax documents and W-2 form, and I asked her if she had childcare for her kids because that's a credit."

It was this simple routine question that opened a door of

opportunity for Lettecia. She and the client started talking about children and it turned out the woman worked for Hope-Link, a nonprofit organization that serves homeless and low-income families, children, seniors, and people with disabilities. The client suggested that the newly single mother of two look into a child-care program they provided just a few miles from Lettecia's office.

"She definitely was like an angel in disguise for me," recalls Lettecia.

At the time, Lettecia was mainly working nights part-time. Because of her break-up, Lettecia knew she was going to have to work full-time in order to support herself and her kids. What she didn't know was how she was going to afford the childcare, and where to find high-quality care on her budget.

That's where the Hope-Link Adelle Maxwell Child Development Center came to the rescue. The Center serves about eighty homeless or low-income children, from infants to eight-year-olds, and charges qualifying low-income families on a sliding scale based on their wages. Funded through a combination of sources including public and private foundations, United Way, government support, and by donations from individuals, organizations and corporations in the community, Hope-Link provides small class sizes with individual learning plans for students. They also provide before- and after-school care, hot meals, on-site medical and mental healthcare, parent education, and a nutrition program. Needless to say, there's often a waiting list for space in this childcare center.

After hearing about the center, Lettecia went in and filled out an application for each of her two sons. "They were really sweet and smart," she recalls of the staff. The in-house childcare advocate helped her apply for a subsidy program though the state. The cost without subsidies was about $1,100 per month, roughly Lettecia's monthly take-home pay. She remarks, "That's pretty much what I was making after taxes." So when Lettecia applied and qualified for a subsidy she ended up only having to pay $350 per month out of pocket.

"It was incredible. It was like, 'Wow, we can eat!' " She notes, "I probably wouldn't have been able to work and would have gone on welfare if not for the subsidies. I just don't know. I hate to think of what would have happened . . ."

Her son Mason started first at the childcare center, while Alex stayed on the waiting list for a while and then started too. Not surprisingly, Lettecia's children are thriving in the preschool. Her son, Mason, at age four is now an avid early reader. At a recent dentist appointment he surprised his mother by reading, "I like to brush my teeth" from a poster in the dental office. The preschool creates an individual curriculum for Mason to keep up with his speedy learning. And Lettecia also feels supported. "They make an effort to help me because they know it's difficult to combine work, going back to school, and being a mom."

This is a prime example of a childcare center that's truly supporting families—a worthy goal for all families. Without the public and private partnerships, extensive funding network, and sliding scale subsidized care, this center with its excellent academic and community programs simply wouldn't exist. Frankly, it doesn't exist for most parents.

Endings and Beginnings

The two-year-old with the mean teacher at the beginning of this chapter is now a nine-year-old with a zest for life. Haylee was a pirate for Halloween this year—one with big black platform shoes, several tangled skull and bone bracelets, pirate shirting, and lipstick (for a new twist on an old image). A quick, intelligent kid, she loves horses, reading, fishing, and all things adventurous. Her mother was able to find a better, yet quite expensive, preschool where Haylee thrived as a little girl. Haylee's story ended well, but too many working families have little choice but to stay in inadequate care. As a nation, we must do better.

With little tasseled graduation caps on their heads and gowns over their clothes, the five-year-old graduates at Angenita's in-home childcare center lined up to show their stuff to parents and classmates. They took turns sharing their prowess in Spanish; sign language; counting by twos, fives, and tens to one hundred; and telling their names and phone numbers. As they each walked up front for their special moment, cameras were flashing, video tapes recording, and the children beamed. The parent of each child came up to the front of the room to publicly congratulate their child on their early success. The room was full of laughter, clapping, and even some tears.

Angenita created a special environment for the children in her care. The story of the obstacles she overcame as an in-home childcare worker is one with huge heart and a hopeful ending. That said: Joining a union to consolidate the workers' collective power is only a beginning. Even with the incremental successes mentioned in Angenita's story, the majority of these in-home childcare workers that care for children forty to sixty hours a week still don't make a living wage, and don't have health insurance. In fact, childcare workers as a whole—from those who work in independent childcare centers to those who work from home—don't have the benefits they need to protect themselves and their families from falling into poverty.

Childcare workers are providing our society with a crucial service. They should not be asked to personally take on an unfair share of the burden of supporting our nation's children. As a country, we must find ways to provide them with benefits and a fair living wage so they can continue to do the work they love, work that is so valuable to their communities and to the economic health of our nation. Community education, organizing, pressure, and support can help change the way childcare workers are compensated, as we saw in Illinois.

Daliyah, four years old, clearly loves going to the military child development center she attends during the day while her mom is working. "When I drop her off, she runs to the teachers and gives them a hug. She always wants to be the last one left because she wants to have more fun," recounts Alberta

LEARNING FROM UNION PROGRAMS

by Netsy Firestein, Director of the Labor Project for Working Families

In 1992, 1199SEIU, representing hospital workers in New York City, negotiated a childcare fund to address the overwhelming need of its' members for high-quality, affordable childcare and services. Today, the 1199 SEIU/Employer childcare Fund (the "Fund") has over 450 employers contributing over thirteen million dollars. The Fund provides benefits to over 10,000 children each year.

The Fund offers the following benefits to its members:

Voucher Reimbursements—Reimbursements to offset the cost of childcare and after-school programs. The reimbursement amount is based on salary, number of dependents and type of care. *(For example, a father earning $28,000 with two children in licensed daycare may receive approximately $845 each quarter.)*

Childcare Resource and Referral Services—Access to counselors who provide referrals for licensed centers, family daycare providers, after-school programs, summer day camps and special-needs programs.

Subsidized Childcare Slots—Slots at licensed childcare centers that are available to members on a sliding fee scale.

with a smile in her voice. "She'll tell me, 'I'm not ready to go home yet. Pick me up last.' So I know my baby's being taken care of."

It's clear to Alberta that the teachers not only care about the kids, but also are on top of their education, "Every time they bring her out, the teachers tell me her progress—the things she learns, what's she's doing," says Alberta.

The military's well-funded child development program enriches the lives of both families and childcare providers. This doesn't happen by chance. The military prioritizes excellent

Workforce 2000—A year-round program for teenagers, designed to help them prepare for college and explore career choices.

Cultural Arts Program and Stipend—Parents who work weekends can place their child in full-day Saturday classes, sponsored by the Fund. Classes include dance, music, theater, and tutoring.

Holiday Program—The Fund contracts with local holiday camps during school breaks throughout the year.

Summer Day Camp—The Fund contracts with 140 local summer day camps for parents to access during the summer holidays.

Summer Camp for Special Needs Children—Parents of children with special needs may enroll their child at a camp of their choosing, appropriate for their child.

Parenting Workshops—The Fund works with universities to provide parenting workshops to 1199 members.

SAT/PSAT Prep Courses—The Fund offers test preparation classes to high school students who are thinking about college.

—Adapted from "A Job and A Life, Organizing and Bargaining for Work Family Issues, A Union Guide". Labor Project for Working Families. Available at www.laborproject.org

childcare, not just with their policies, but with funding: For example, in 2004 the Department of Defense budgeted $379 million to support serving over 200,000 children, not including additional supplemental funds.[32] A majority of problems with the civilian childcare picture come back to a shortage of funding—funding to help parents that need assistance, funding for providers' salaries and education, and funding for educational resources. It is penny wise and pound foolish to underfund childcare.

Lettecia doesn't know what she would do without Hope-Link's

TAKING CARE OF OUR OWN—UNIONS IN ACTION

by Netsy Firestein, Director of the Labor Project for Working Families

UNITE HERE Local 2 represents approximately 12,000 hotel and restaurant workers in San Francisco. In 1994, the union and San Francisco's union hotels successfully negotiated a fund, paid by employers, to help offset the child and elder care costs of their members, known as the Local 2/Hospitality Industry Child and Elder Care Plan. The hotel business is a 24-hour service industry with jobs being traditionally low paid, and so the Fund has made a significant difference to the lives of many Local 2 members.

The Plan offers the following benefits:

Elder Care—Monthly subsidy to help offset the cost of health-related services for an elderly parent, parent-in-law, grandparent, or a disabled child, spouse or domestic partner.

Newborn—Monthly subsidy to parents of newborns during the baby's first year.

Pre-Kinder childcare—Monthly subsidy to offset the cost of licensed childcare for parents with children who are not yet attending kindergarten.

Formal childcare—A stipend to help pay for licensed childcare for children up to the age of thirteen. This includes after-school programs.

Informal childcare—A monthly subsidy to pay for informal childcare

Adelle Maxwell Child Development Center that provides excellent care for her sons while taking into account what she and her family can afford. Her sons Mason, four years old, and Alex, three years old, are blossoming in the center. Knowing her children are in good care, Lettecia is going back to school herself to get a nursing degree while also working. This is so she can eventually bring in more money to support her family. Clearly, the children are thriving, and so is their mother. Without the subsidized provider, often a relative or friend (this is less money than formal care to encourage use of formal care).

Youth Program—Subsidy for expenses such as summer camp, music lessons or other kinds of enrichment classes. This benefit covers children up to the age of eighteen.

SAT College Prep Course—A free SAT college prep course is available to the high school children of Local 2 members. The parents are invited to an SAT orientation session and a financial aid workshop at the end of the course.

Elder Care Resource and Referral Service—Access to counselors who provide information on state and local assistance programs as well as referrals for caregivers and centers within the community.

Hospital workers, auto workers, clerical workers and communications workers all have unions that have negotiated for vital programs to help workers' families—subsidies for newborns and toddler childcare, homework hotlines for older kids, limits on mandatory overtime, day at a time vacations and flextime have all been negotiated to support good parenting.

—Adapted from "A Job and A Life, Organizing and Bargaining for Work Family Issues, A Union Guide". Labor Project for Working Families. Available at www.laborproject.org

childcare, this family, like many others, would likely stay stuck in a cycle of poverty.

The stories of local subsidized childcare through Hope-Link, and that of the military childcare program, are two examples of success from which we can learn. It's time to work to ensure that all children and families have access to excellent childcare.

The current childcare landscape is diverse and reflects the creativity of parents under pressure—parent co-ops where parents take turns watching groups of children, internet matching of childcare needs, so parents can share the cost of childcare providers, union-sponsored or negotiated childcare, company-provided childcare, more access to quality emergency backup daycare in some areas, and an increasing understanding that some working parents need care for children after 6 P.M. as they work nontraditional schedules.

Yet there aren't many easy answers or quick solutions, notes Netsy Firestein, Director of the Labor Project for Working Families. "Some of these options are complicated, particularly because the root of the problem is allowing parents the time they need to parent. So for example, instead of backup sick care for children, we as a society should make sure people have paid sick days for when they need to care for their child or other family members. Some of this can be solved through flexible schedules, but some workers don't get that option because of their type of job." She concludes, "It's striking a balance between living in a 24/7 economy and being able to raise a family. If we want people to work different shifts and weekends, then we have to come up with better solutions for people to be able to care for families." Ultimately, we need to address the fact that as a nation we must prioritize supporting the care of our young children.

Setting Priorities

Top quality childcare is a fundamental requirement for our children's academic and emotional development. With this in mind, we must do two things:

1. Make quality, accessible, and affordable childcare available to all parents.

2. Give childcare providers training, a living wage, and benefits in order to attract and retain excellent childcare workers.

Parents and children suffer when childcare is substandard. Early childhood education is a huge opportunity for us to advance the success of children, and to support working parents. When children are put into childcare that amounts to a holding tank, those children lose precious opportunities to develop socially and academically, and we all are diminished as a result. Parents and children need more community support for early care and education; it is smart to invest in our future.

Chapter "E"—Excellent Childcare.

It is a reality of modern life that most mothers need to reenter the workforce before their children are in elementary school. Moreover, many mothers cannot depend on relatives to help. Mothers need high-quality, nurturing childcare to ensure that children are safe, well cared for, and ready for school. America must invest in early care, not just because necessary for mothers and kids, but because each child is precious to society as a whole—they represent the future productive engine of our economy.

ACTION: Mothers want—

(1)   Quality, affordable Childcare that is available to all parents who need it.

(2)   Childcare providers who are paid at least a living wage and healthcare benefits.

(3)   Programs to ensure that education and training opportunities are available to childcare providers, and childcare providers' compensation should be increased commensurate with their education.

To share your story, go to **www.MotherhoodManifesto.com.**

7

Realistic and Fair Wages

Audrey, wearing her veterinarian's lab coat, walked into the examination room where a large, lethargic, primarily white cat with orange tabby coloring named Boomer was resting on the metal examination table. The animal technicians had already come in and taken Boomer's temperature, pulse, and blood pressure. Audrey reviewed their findings on the chart before she walked into the room to find Boomer's owners hovering nervously next to the table.

Audrey got her degree at the University of Pennsylvania,

MOTHERS AND NON-MOTHERS

A recent study found that mothers were 44 percent less likely to be hired than non-mothers for the same job given the exact same resume and experience for the two groups of women (mothers and non-mothers). And non-mothers were offered an average of $11,000 more than mothers for that same high-salaried job.[38]

School of Veterinary Medicine, one of the top veterinary schools in the country, in 1993. An experienced veterinarian, she picked up Boomer and expertly examined him starting with his head and moving all the way down his body to his tail. The owners told her that Boomer hadn't been eating, had been drinking lots of water, and generally didn't seem to be feeling well. They adored their feline companion of more than a decade and were worried about what was going on with him.

Audrey had her suspicions, so she took some blood work to run a panel of diagnostic tests and told them she'd get back to them the next day. This was just one appointment of a series of back-to-back thirty-minute appointments that started at 8:30 A.M. and ended at 6:30 P.M.

As Audrey did her work with the animals, another veterinarian with similar education and work experience was also seeing animals in the same clinic. They worked side by side, doing essentially the same job. But there was one big difference: the pay.

Audrey, the mother of two elementary school-aged daughters, was making a couple of dollars less per hour than her co-worker who, while also a woman, didn't have any children. Not a lot of money per hour, but the total wage loss adds up over time.

Audrey's experience puts a face to the statistics that show, on the whole, non-mothers make more than mothers. It's not just Audrey in this predicament, and it's not just faceless "big businesses" that have a part in this discrimination. This scenario plays out across the country on a daily basis. "She was doing the same job and had the same education and experience," recalls Audrey, "and we had a boss who was also a woman who didn't have children, and the whole dynamic was horrible."

As we've discussed through this book, women like Audrey aren't just imagining that the wage discrimination they experience in the workforce may be related to them being mothers. Here it is front and center again: We face growing wage gaps between mothers and non-mothers (in 1991, non-mothers with an average age of thirty made 90 cents to a man's dollar, while moms made only 73 cents to the dollar, and single moms made 56 to 66 cents to a man's dollar).[1] And this maternal pay gap has been growing. The pay gap between mothers and non-mothers actually expanded from 10 percent in 1980 to 17.5 percent in 1991.[2]

Yes, it's with motherhood—a time when families need more economic support for basic needs, childcare, and healthcare; not less support—that women take the biggest economic hits in the form of lower pay. And, it's also with motherhood that some clues appear as to how the wage gap can be narrowed.

Dr. Shelley Correll's groundbreaking research released in 2005 is a compelling addition to the long line of studies that explore the roots of this maternal wage gap. This study, like others, also found that the wage gap wasn't linked to self-limiting factors that might cause a wage gap, like mothers taking more time off to care for children, but in actuality is fairly straightforward discrimination. In other words, it's not mothers' "fault" they receive less pay.

The basic findings: Mothers are 44 percent less likely to be hired than non-mothers for the same job given the exact same resume and experience for the two groups of women (mothers and non-mothers). Her study also found that mothers are offered significantly lower starting pay. Study participants offered non-mothers an average of $11,000 more than mothers for the same high salaried job as equally qualified non-mothers.[3]

"We expected to find that moms were going to be discriminated against, but I was surprised by the magnitude of the gap," comments Dr. Correll. "I expected small numbers but we found huge numbers. Another thing was that fathers were actually advantaged and we didn't expect fathers to be offered more money or to be rated higher." But that's what happened. A study by Jane Waldfogel of Columbia University, published in the *Journal of Economic Perspectives,* found the same thing: Men don't take wage hits after having children, women do.[4]

Critics often assume that the mothers studied tended to have less education or work experience than non-mothers, thus skewing the findings; yet the Waldfogel study filtered the data to account for education and work experience,[5] and the Correll study had equal resumes so there weren't any differences in education and work experience. Something is really going on here.

And that "something" has a tremendous impact on poverty rates for women and families. Women in low-wage jobs are not advancing up and out of those positions at the same rate as men,[6] and women in high-wage jobs are being offered less pay. The Institute for Women's Policy Research, notes, "We did a study that found if there wasn't a wage gap, the poverty rates for single moms would be cut in half, and the poverty rates for dual earner families would be cut by about 25 percent."

This brings us to the heart of the matter—and to some ideas for solutions. Waldfogel writes in *The Journal of Economic Perspectives* that one reason for the widening American maternal wage gap "may be the institutional structure in the United States, which has emphasized equal pay and equal opportunity policies, but not family policies such as maternity leave and childcare. Other industrialized countries that have implemented family policies along with their gender policies seem to have had better success at narrowing both the gender gap and the family gap."[7] Family policies such as paid family leave, as well as subsidized child and universal healthcare, have been shown to help close the maternal gap in other countries. Flexible work options that include all men and women (so those that use the flexible work options aren't marginalized) are also important.

Audrey eventually quit the job she held at that veterinary clinic, and took a job where being a mother wasn't a liability. It made all the difference in the world, and she is very happy with her job now—and in fact is better paid, "I'm at a kid friendly clinic now. I have a boss who has children and she's the primary breadwinner. Her husband is staying home with the kids. It's so different, they understand flexibility of scheduling and that if my child is sick then I might need to call and switch coverage with another veterinarian. They understand that if you come to a meeting on your day off, then you may need to bring your child—and they'll pick a kid friendly restaurant to go to for that meeting. None of these things were available at the other place I worked."

There is some variation among like-minded thinkers about what to do first to close the wage gap. Heather Boushey, economist at the Center for Economic and Policy Research notes that flexible work options need to be addressed in order to close the wage gap. "There are so many different layers to women's pay issues. On the one hand, there is the pay equity question. But there is also this question about valuing care and allowing workers to provide care for their family members. So if you want to equalize the labor market then you have to find some way to address this issue—either by offering paid leave to both women and men—and increasing the propensity of men taking that leave—or by finding some other way to reduce the penalties for breaks in employment."

Marsha Meyer, a professor at the School of Social Work, University of Washington, and co-author of *Families That Work*, agrees, and adds, "Many people say that it should be okay for women to work as many long hours as men, not take career breaks with kids, and to put in long enough hours to be CEOs, tenured professors, and partners in law firms, but what we argue in our book is that this solution ignores kids, and ignores the social benefits we all get from someone taking care of kids. It's not just women working more hours, but men being able to have the flexibility and incentives to take care of kids as well." Otherwise, she comments, what happens is that women end up taking all the leave because they often have lower salaries than their husbands, which makes it economically smarter for families to live on the higher salary. If this pattern keeps repeating, then the wage gap doesn't close, Meyer argues, but is reinforced.

In the end, maternal bias is a reality we must address if we value both fair treatment in the workplace and the contributions working mothers make to our economy. No matter which policy area is worked on first, there's little question that paid family leave for both parents, flexible work options, access to quality healthcare, affordable childcare, and realistic wages are all tied together and need to be brought front and center in our national conversation. The motherhood wage gap needs to be closed.

Vicky Lovell, Study Director at the Institute for Women's Policy Research, ties it all together. "Families can't function well if they don't have adequate income. And if people don't have pay that is high enough, then they may have to take jobs that aren't workable for them because they are too far away from home for them to have time to see their children, they may put off preventative healthcare, or even put off trips to the emergency room, or struggle with finding adequate childcare. To be family-friendly we have to provide holistic supports for the entire family. Economic security is part of being able to care for your family."

The root of economic security starts with being able to make a high enough wage to afford basic food, housing, healthcare, and other living necessities. Many families are struggling with minimum and very low wage jobs that frankly don't provide a living wage. This impacts women, mothers in particular, more than others because they are less likely to move up and out of minimum wage positions over time,[8] and are paid less than men on the whole. Gender as well as maternal discrimination and low-wage jobs are linked. Working to raise the bar of wage floors is particularly helpful to women and children. In fact, a report found a majority of the employees who would benefit from an increased minimum wage (62 percent) are women.[9]

Minimum Wage, Maximum Problems

Mindy, six months pregnant, worked the 6 A.M. through 2 P.M. shift as a waitress. It was so busy that on many days she didn't get a chance to stop and eat. Sometimes she'd put a plate of French fries out in the kitchen so she could pop one in her mouth as she rushed by to pick up a soda order. She was on her feet for eight hours every day, and by the time Mindy was at the end of her second trimester, she was thoroughly fatigued. At about that time, Mindy almost fainted at work. So she sat down for a moment in the restaurant to pull herself together, and a person at one of her tables didn't miss a beat, calling out, "Ma'm, we still need our coffee."

At that time, she and her husband Ruben had three jobs between them—Mindy with one job, and, Ruben, with two. All three jobs were paid minimum wage. Even with tips, making ends meet was a struggle. Mindy worked through most of her first pregnancy at a restaurant in downtown San Francisco. It was a long slender room, almost like a train car, with eleven booths and twenty counter seats. Decorated in red and white, with James Dean and Marilyn Monroe looking down from their spots on the walls, this was a major tourist attraction and had a high traffic flow of people from all over the world stopping in for a bite to eat.

Mindy's body was getting stressed from the fatigue and her doctor wrote her a note that specified she needed regular breaks. "It was the constant motion and the duration of not getting enough food," she comments about working through her pregnancy. "And the baby was growing erratically; she wasn't steadily increasing in size. The doctor said, 'Your body is stressed and your baby is showing signs of that stress.'"

Mindy didn't have healthcare through her job, but was able to see the doctor because she qualified for health insurance through a state of California low-income insurance program called Access for Infants and Mothers (AIM), "It was pregnancy

MINIMUM WAGE

by Madeline Janis-Aparicio, Executive Director, Los Angeles Alliance for a New
Economy, and Jessica Goodheart, Co-Director of Research, Los Angeles Alliance
for a New Economy

Established in 1938 as part of the Fair Labor Standards Act, the federal
minimum wage was intended to provide workers with a minimum standard of living. The basic notion—supported by the majority of Americans—is that a decent day's work deserves a decent day's pay.

However, the minimum wage—$5.15 per hour—is not enough to
keep even the smallest family above the federal government's extremely
low poverty threshold. Furthermore, its value has been declining over
time. The real value of the federal minimum wage in 1968 was $7.54,
46 percent more than the current hourly minimum of $5.15. A full-time
worker earning the minimum wage would bring home only $10,712. In

specific insurance, so I was covered for the entire pregnancy and
for two months after giving birth. The baby is covered for the
first year of life."

She found out about this state health insurance program when
she went into a clinic for a pregnancy test to confirm the test she
took at home. It was a walk-in clinic that she came across on an
advertisement on the bathroom wall at work. "The advertisement
said, 'Think you're pregnant? Come in to get a verification test and
find out about your different options,' " recalls Mindy, "But we
already knew we wanted to keep the baby," and just wanted to confirm the pregnancy. This clinic helped Mindy apply for the AIM
healthcare program and also got her in touch with the WIC office
to help with food. WIC is the Special Supplemental Nutrition

addition, the minimum wage, which is not adjusted for inflation, does not reflect rising costs of housing, healthcare and—with women increasingly a part of the workforce—childcare.

Opponents of minimum wage increases argue that they merely impact teenagers who are not the primary earners in their family. But the ten million or so minimum wage workers contribute—on average—54 percent to their family's weekly earnings. Most of these workers (58 percent) are women, and the vast majority (71 percent) are twenty or over.

In addition, opponents argue that minimum wage increases cause job losses, harming the very workers they are intended to help. However, economists have studied the question extensively in New Jersey and other states that have raised the minimum wage, and found no evidence that modest minimum wage increases cause job loss. The stagnation of the federal minimum wage has prompted states, local governments, and even universities to establish minimum wage standards that better reflect the idea that workers deserve a living wage.

Program for Women, Infants, and Children, a federal government assistance program that provides nutritious food to qualifying low-income women, infants, and children up to age five.[10]

Without this subsidized help, Mindy and her family wouldn't have had healthcare coverage, and would have struggled to pay for food with just the earnings from their minimum wage jobs. She was working so hard to keep up with the bills that the fatigue was complicating her pregnancy.

Mindy ended up having to take early maternity leave, and even then had to have an emergency C-section because her amniotic fluid was so low. "Luckily, she's fine now," says Mindy who later had to quit her job to care for her own health, as well as to take care of her daughter, then later also for her son. At the time it also made economic sense for Mindy to stay home with their children—childcare costs would have dwarfed her minimum wage salary. "I couldn't afford childcare while I worked. I just didn't make enough," says Mindy. "If there was some type of childcare assistance program through work or the state then I could have worked."

Losing Mindy's wages was a big blow. The wages of two parents are often needed to support a family these days. When those wages are not adequate to cover the costs of raising children and other basic needs like housing, heat, utilities, groceries, childcare, clothing, health coverage, and transportation costs, then we have a significant problem. Raising the minimum will better allow families to meet those needs on their own.[11]

Mindy's family ended up struggling to make ends meet on just the wages her husband brought in from his two minimum wage jobs. Her situation with one parent making minimum wage to support a family isn't rare. In fact, "the average minimum wage worker brings home more than half (54 percent) of his or her family's weekly earnings," finds the Economic Policy Institute.[12]

One of her husband's jobs was at a cozy sidewalk café, the kind where BLTs cost $9, and the hamburgers come with freshly cut fruit instead of French fries. There were six or seven outdoor tables, and a small interior with five or six tables on the first floor and a narrow staircase up to a few more tables. The walls were covered with the pictures, sometimes autographed, of famous people who had dined at the restaurant. For an added touch of class, each table had a small vase with a flower. The restaurant shared the street with expensive stores like Giorgio Armani, BCBG, Kenneth Cole, and local upscale boutiques.

> **FEDERAL MINIMUM WAGE**
>
> By working a 52-week full-time job without unpaid breaks, the federal minimum wage comes to $10,712 per year.

The people who worked in the restaurant, however, couldn't afford to shop at those stores. Ruben, Mindy's husband, now the sole wage earner in his family of three—nearly four—was struggling to support his family as he brought home minimum wage and tips for his work as a waiter. He also had a second job waiting tables at another restaurant, where he was paid minimum wage as well. At that time, San Francisco was one of the few cities which passed a minimum wage increase within their city limits. The city had a minimum wage of $8.50 per hour,[13] which is significantly higher than the $5.15 per hour federal minimum wage.[14]

In fact, there's been some movement to raise the minimum wage in cities and states across the country through citizen initiatives, state legislatures, and other elected bodies. Several cities—like San Francisco—have successfully raised the minimum wage within their city limits, and fifteen states have minimum wages that are higher than the federal government's $5.15 an hour.[15] Florida, with a minimum wage in 2005 of $6.15 per hour, is one of those states.[16] Their minimum wage increase was voted in by citizens who also voted for George Bush for President in 2004. Clearly, this is not a partisan issue.

A RISING TIDE OF ECONOMIC INSECURITY

by Jacob S. Hacker, Ph.D., Peter Strauss Family
Associate Professor, Yale University

Everyone knows economic *inequality* has increased dramatically. Less well known is that economic *insecurity* has increased even more dramatically. Since the early 1970s, the year-to-year instability of family incomes has skyrocketed, even as middle-class incomes have risen only modestly.

The signs of this "great risk shift" are everywhere. Personal bankruptcy rates have increased fivefold in the last quarter century, to roughly 1.5 million. The mortgage foreclosure rate has increased threefold, and family debt is at record levels. Meanwhile, employers have shifted from so-called defined-benefit pensions that promise a fixed benefit in retirement toward "defined-contribution" pensions, like 401(k)s, that greatly increase the degree of risk placed on individual workers.

For more than a decade, moreover, the ranks of the medically

It's hard for a family to live on minimum wages. The cost of living is just too high. Contrary to popular belief, the majority of minimum wage earners aren't single teenagers who need to bring in a little extra for pocket change, many families struggle with these issues: A report found that 70 percent of workers who would benefit from an increased minimum wage are adults age twenty or older.[17]

No, these aren't just teenagers with summer jobs.

While Ruben was juggling his two jobs, he and Mindy were also raising their daughter, Kennedy, and Mindy became pregnant with their second child. What did living on the minimum uninsured have expanded with little interruption. Over a two-year period, one in three nonelderly Americans spend some time without health coverage. In 2004, more than 14 million nonelderly Americans paid more than a quarter of their earnings on medical costs and premiums. And health costs and crises are a factor in nearly half of all personal bankruptcies.

Economic insecurity hits women, minorities, and the less well educated hardest, because their incomes fluctuate the most and they are least likely to have access to job-based benefits. Yet insecurity has worsened rapidly across nearly every segment of American society. It is a common problem that can and should be the basis for common solutions.

Yet, under the banner of "the ownership society," many conservative politicians are calling for measures that will actually make Americans more insecure—measures like private accounts in Social Security that will shift even greater risk onto Americans' already burdened shoulders. America's hardworking families need stronger floodwalls against the rising tide of economic insecurity, not to have those floodwalls torn down.

wages of one earner (holding two jobs) mean for her family? "We couldn't buy the groceries we wanted. We were cutting back on fruits and vegetables because they are the most expensive. Actually, we were living mostly on WIC items, like the cheese, eggs, and milk."

The current federal minimum wage is the result of the last increase in 1996–97 (It was a stepped wage increase—with part of the increase in 1996 and the second part in 1997). Between the time the minimum wage was last raised and 2005, inflation has worn down the wage value: The $5.15 per hour in 2005 is equivalent to $4.23 per hour in 1995.[18] The minimum wage is actually losing ground over time. And, it's abundantly clear that few adults can get by on the federal minimum wage without public assistance of some kind.

More women than men are stuck in minimum and low-wage jobs. In fact, a 2005 study found that between 1992 and 2003, 41 percent of women remained in low-wage jobs, compared to only 34 percent of men (48 percent of men moved up to an above-wage job during that time period, and only 32 percent of women made the jump up).[19] Stagnant minimum wage rates enable employers to pay the lowest rates to our most vulnerable citizens. In the end, there's little question that mothers are among the most vulnerable workers in our society, making an average of 24 percent less than men.[20]

Nuts and Bolts—A Living Wage

Calculations back up the sentiment that $5.15 per hour isn't enough to support a family—$5.15 simply doesn't meet the Self-Sufficiency Standard, which calculates how much money working adults need to meet their basic needs without any subsidies of any kind.[21] Taking San Francisco as an example, the hourly Self-Sufficiency Standard wage rate needed by two working adults to support themselves, along with a preschool age child and a child in school, has been calculated at $14.27 per hour per adult.[22]

The federal minimum wage is currently so far from being high enough to provide people with sufficient money to meet basic needs, that many are taking the fight for fair wages to their own backyards by working on local living wage campaigns. Across the country advocates are working hard in local jurisdictions.

Stephanie Luce, who teaches in the University of Massachusetts' Labor Studies department, explains it this way: "The United States is the richest country in the history of the world and yet a quarter to a third of American workers work for an hourly wage that is not enough for them to meet the federal poverty line. So we're talking up to 40 million workers earning quite low wages because we know that even the federal poverty line has been judged by experts to be too low to accurately judge poverty. The living wage movement is basically a movement of campaigns run by community and labor groups to raise wages for workers through legislation, initiatives, contract negotiations, and any other avenue open to workers."

These living wage campaigns often work through local governments to pass standards that say, for example, city governments will set a floor for their wages that is closer to a living wage, and will only work with contractors that pay a living wage. Dr. Luce comments, "In my research, I've come up with a rough estimate that suggests workers have received three quarters of a billion dollars in wage increases through these efforts in 130 cities." For instance, after a campaign for the city of San Francisco to pay living wages to their contractors and leaseholders, changes were made with the workers at the San Francisco International Airport when they adopted a Quality Standards

POSITIVE BUSINESS RESULTS FROM INCREASED WAGES
• Lower turnover
• Fewer disciplinary problems
• Improved job performance
• Lower recruiting and training costs
• Decline in absenteeism

Program that set wage floors (otherwise known as a minimum wage) for contractors. This was a big improvement in the pay scale of people who worked for the city at the airport.

Here's what happened: The national average pay for preboarding airport security screeners was $6 per hour, and those security jobs had extremely high turnover rates (the national average turnover was 125 percent in 1999)—jeopardizing what the job is meant to do, which is provide security.[23] The pay floor was increased to $10 per hour if they received benefits and to $11.25 per hour if they didn't have benefits.[24]

This new pay floor at the airport made a huge difference, improving both airport security performance and lives of the workers at the same time. A study of the impact of that living wage pay raise found that annual turnover of airport security workers dropped from 110 percent to 25 percent, and one security contracting firm reported in an even lower 15 percent turnover. The study also found improved job performance with a decline in absenteeism, as well as in disciplinary problems.[25] The cost of this living wage program was estimated to be a small $1.37 price increase to airline passengers.[26] That cost, compared to the benefits workers gained and improved airport security performance, makes changes like these no-brainers.

The Minimum Wage Debate

Increasing the minimum wage will substantially improve the living standards for many women and families. Why hasn't it been done yet? Why the delay from 1997? One answer is that a debate rages about whether or not increasing the minimum wage will hurt businesses and cause them to cut back on available jobs. Yet several studies show that raising the minimum wage does not cause overall job loss. One study, published in *The American Economic Review*, tracked the impact of the minimum wage increase by the state of New Jersey in the fast-food industry and found, "no evidence that the rise in New Jersey's minimum wage reduced employment in fast-food restaurants in the state."[27]

A different study, released in 2004, did a comparison between states with the federal minimum wage of $5.15 per hour, and those that have passed a higher minimum wage to see if there was any impact on small businesses.[28] This study found that small business job growth in the states with an increased minimum wage was actually higher than in states that have the lower federal minimum wage, and that small businesses with fifty or fewer employees weren't hurt by the state minimum wage increases. To the contrary, the report notes, "using the latest Commerce Department data, employment and payroll growth in the higher minimum wage states performed better than in the remaining states."[29]

In addition, a study of the previously mentioned living wage increase at the San Francisco airport found that businesses realize savings through lower turnover, recruiting and training costs, fewer disciplinary problems, and a more engaged workforce.

Mothers comprise a substantial portion of the citizens struggling to live on minimum wage. "An analysis of low-wage workers shows that the main beneficiaries of this one-dollar increase [from $5.15 an hour to $6.15] would be working women, almost one million of whom are single mothers," found a study published by the Economic Policy Institute. "In fact, of the 11.8 million workers who would receive a pay increase as the result of this higher minimum wage, 58 percent would be women, simply because, as a group, they earn lower wages than men. As a result, a minimum wage increase would help to reduce the overall pay gap between women and men."[30]

A federal minimum wage increase will improve the lives of working mothers more than most for two reasons: Women are more likely to be stuck in minimum wage jobs, and mothers on average earn lower wages than non-mothers and men. The federal minimum wage must be raised.

Low-Wage Work

Diane, a mother of three, was standing in the prep room of the Wal-Mart deli where she worked in Florida. The room was sparsely set up with a big double sink, walk-in cooler, freezer, a couple of preparation tables, and a hand-washing sink. Regulation white walls, a double door to the warehouse, and a single swinging door to the customer area completed the twenty-five-square foot concrete-floored room.

She and two other women who worked together at the deli were getting ready for the day, taking food out of the freezer, opening packages of meat, and putting together food trays. A young man about eighteen years old, a new hire, walked through the double swinging doors from the warehouse muttering complaints under his breath. Diane recalls, "He was saying, 'They want me to do this, and they want me to do that, all for this small amount of money. And then he said his pay.' We were all like, 'What! That's how much they hired you at!?'" His pay was much higher than theirs.

When hired, all the women were told it was store policy to start everyone at the same wage of $6.50 per hour. And the women knew for a fact that another recent hire in their department, a woman with eleven years experience, was hired at that rate (as were they). When they accidentally found out the young man was hired for quite a bit more, the women were upset.

Like Diane, they were all mothers who dearly needed their wages to support their children and families. They were more than upset; they were outraged.

Gender inequality in the workplace is far from a thing of the past.

Despite the data that shows wage gaps, some question whether or not wage inequalities between men and women still exist. Societal trends are easier to see when large numbers of workers' wages are considered at the same time. So let's look at the company where Diane works, Wal-Mart, which is our nation's largest private employer. Wal-Mart has more than 3,000 stores around the country, and as many as 1.6 million women have worked for Wal-Mart since 1998.

In 2001, six current and former female Wal-Mart employees filed a national sex-discrimination class-action lawsuit, alleging widespread gender bias against women with regard to pay, job assignments, and promotions. This lawsuit, *Dukes v. Wal-Mart Stores, Inc.*, is ongoing and active. According to a statistical report prepared by Dr. Richard Drogin, the plaintiffs' expert in the Wal-Mart case, "Women employees at Wal-Mart are concentrated in the lower paying jobs, are paid less than men in the same jobs and are less likely to advance to management positions

WAL-MART ON TRIAL

by Irma Herrera, Executive Director, Equal Rights Advocates, Inc.

In June 2001 Betty Dukes and five other current and former employees of Wal-Mart filed a lawsuit on behalf of themselves and a class of other women workers charging Wal-Mart with systematically discriminating against its female employees in promotions, compensation, and training in its over 3,300 Wal-Mart and Sam's Club retail stores nationwide in violation of federal anti-discrimination law (Title VII of the Civil Rights Act of 1964).

In support of their Motion to Certify the Class, plaintiffs provided sworn testimony from women who worked in 184 Wal-Mart stores in than men. These gender patterns persist even though women have more seniority, have lower turnover rates, and have higher performance ratings in most jobs."

Diane and her co-workers aren't part of that lawsuit. For many Wal-Mart workers, lawsuits seem remote, and they don't want to complicate their lives, which are already too demanding. What they did do after accidentally uncovering wage inequality was ask for a meeting with the store manager.

On the day they asked for the meeting they searched all over the store for the manager and couldn't find him. Finally, towards the end of the day, they were called into the manager's office. He was absent, but in his place were four men from the main management division. There was only one other woman invited to the meeting, and she was from the personnel office.

The division managers were all sitting around a conference

thirty different states around the country, as well as the depositions of more than 100 Wal-Mart managers and executives whose testimony was taken under oath and from payroll data and over 1,200,000 pages of documents produced by Wal-Mart from it's corporate files.

Wal-Mart's own workforce data revealed that women in every major job category at Wal-Mart have been paid less than men with the same seniority in every year since 1997, even though female employees on average have higher performance ratings and less turnover than men. Wal-Mart's internal documents also acknowledged that the corporation was "behind the rest of the world" in the promotion of women.

Wal-Mart appealed the class certification to the Ninth Circuit Court of Appeals, and arguments on the appeal were heard in August 2005. As of the end of 2005, the Ninth Circuit had not yet issued a decision.

room table on cold metal chairs when Diane and her co-workers walked in. There was an empty desk at the end of the room, and for some odd reason the main decorative feature of the office was a life-size cutout of a racecar driver. The women sat down and were "yelled at" by the managers: "We were told if we were ever caught discussing our pay again it was grounds for termination. They were very agitated and weren't sympathetic at all. It was like we did something wrong. But we never even asked about pay, he just came out and said it. All we ever wanted to do was talk to the store manager and we never got to," recalls Diane.

Diane later found out that under Florida law, discussing pay is not grounds for termination, as it is in many states. In a recent

THE LEGAL SYSTEM IN ACTION

by Professor Joan Williams, Director of Center for WorkLife Law
at U.C. Hastings College of Law, and Donna Norton, Esq.,
Consultant to the Center for WorkLife Law

Like Kiki, the single mother of two who faced repeated discrimination while looking for a job, many mothers continue to face bias at the workplace. More and more, women are beginning to use the legal system to fight this discrimination. For example, one woman sued when her employer said that he didn't believe mothers should work because "I don't see how you can do either job well." Another sued after being fired because "she was no longer dependable since she had a child." We've all heard about the glass ceiling, but many women are stopped long before by the "maternal wall."

Maternal wall lawsuits have increased 300 percent since 2000, as compared to the prior five years. In one case, a female civil engineer phone conversation, Amy Caiazza, from The Institute for Women's Policy Research, shared her thoughts from a national perspective: "Right now, in many instances, you can be fired for disclosing your salary. That means most people don't know what their co-workers are making. It's generally very difficult to know whether you are being discriminated against."

Caiazza offers a solution to the problem. "There is a bill on Capital Hill that would protect people so they won't be fired for talking about how much money they make. The bill also requires companies to analyze their salaries and wages and to disclose that data so potential patterns of discrimination can be seen. This is a very simple thing to do."

was awarded $3 million because she was passed over for promotions after the birth of her son. She testified that she was given a choice between the career track and the mommy track when the president of the company asked her, "Do you want to have babies or do you want a career here?"

Currently, mothers are suing under a patchwork of laws, and their success depends on the laws of their state and the views of the court that decides their case. The employment discrimination section of the District of Columbia Human Rights Act is the only state statute that specifically prohibits discrimination against employees on the basis of "family responsibilities." What is needed are state and federal laws that specifically forbid discrimination against mothers and other employees with family caregiving responsibilities. This will not only protect the rights of mothers and other caregivers, but also help employers by clearly defining what policies and practices are legal.

It's often difficult for individuals to see gendered wage inequality. Generally, people don't compare their paychecks at the water fountain, and questioning why one person makes more than another is far from common. That's why comparing wages in large corporations like Wal-Mart is so very revealing about our current status.

So what, you might be wondering, does the wage gap between men and women have to do with motherhood? A close look at the numbers shows that the reason the wage gap is so large for all women is that the vast majority of women become mothers (82 percent).[31] This majority of American women—mothers—are actually making less than the current average reported by the U.S. Census of 76 cents to a man's dollar,[32] since the wages of non-mothers bring up the overall average.

In fact, as we've noted, right now the wage gap between mothers and non-mothers is greater than between women and men—and it's actually getting bigger. Non-mothers earn 10 percent less than their male counterparts; mothers earn 27 percent less; and single mothers earn between 34 percent and 44 percent less.[33] The wage gap, to a large degree, is therefore a direct reflection of bias against working mothers. This bias, in part, is because we don't have family-friendly policies to support the needs of working mothers and families, like flexible work options, paid family leave, and accessible childcare.

But even if we put gender inequality aside (and that's one heck of a big aside), there's something terribly amiss when the nation's largest employer has a significant number of employees needing, and qualifying for, food stamps and other government subsidies in order to support their families while working full-time. This scenario of full-time Wal-Mart workers on public assistance is playing out in states across the nation, which means taxpayers are subsidizing Wal-Mart's profits.

Diane's starting wage of $6.50 per hour adds up to $13,520 per year if she doesn't take any unpaid time off and works all fifty-two weeks of the year at our nation's largest employer. Very few families can live on $13,520 per year.

In blinding contrast, Wal-Mart CEO and President, H. Lee Scott Jr. made $22, 991,599 in 2004.[34] Yes, that's nearly $23 million. It is clear from the CEO's salary that Wal-Mart does not pay low wages to its regular workers because it's struggling to make a profit, but because it's good for investors and the top management. Taxpayers shouldn't have to subsidize thriving businesses.

Time for a Change

As of the writing of this book it has been almost a decade since the federal minimum wage was raised. Every year the cost of living has risen and workers at the bottom pay levels have less purchasing power. It is no coincidence that the number of working poor is growing. In fact, food stamps, subsidized housing, government sponsored healthcare programs, and other government programs for the poor are now a crucial resource for a large numbers of hardworking adults who have full-time low- wage employment. Many of these programs were originally conceived for citizens who lost their jobs, not for those with jobs.

While real wages for low and median-wage employees has remained stagnant or fallen, CEO pay has risen at an astronomical rate. In 1980, CEOs were paid about forty times as much as an ordinary employee. Now it's not unusual for CEO pay to be 500 times as much as the pay of an ordinary employee.[35]

The growing gap between the rich and poor is ultimately not good for our nation. In the last twenty-five years our nation has changed in ways that should cause us concern. In 1968, GM was one of the largest employers in the U.S., paying employees an average of about $29,000 per year (amount adjusted for today's dollars) with excellent benefits.[36] Today Wal-Mart is the biggest employer in the U.S., paying the average full-time worker about $17,000 per year with very poor benefits.[37]

America prides itself on being a land of opportunity, where hard work earns the comfort and security that is the American dream. Better still, a common American dream is to raise your children so their success exceeds your own. It is a good dream, and one we don't want to

---

CEO WAGE RATIOS OFF

"One way to measure hierarchy in a society such as ours is to look at how much CEO's are paid compared to ordinary workers. In the U.S., they are paid about 500 times as much (up from a 40 to one ratio in 1980). In no other country today is the ratio bigger than 50 to one. In Western Europe, Canada, and Japan, CEOs make 20 to 30 times what the average worker makes, and often less."

from the essay by Stephen Bezruchka, titled "The (Bigger) Picture of Health," published in the book, *Take Back Your Time.*

loose. A large educated middle class makes our country strong. We don't want to become a nation of winners and losers, rich and poor, yet the data shows us moving in this direction. Our government is an entity that has some key opportunities to level the playing field for citizens that are struggling. One of those opportunities is raising the federal minimum wage.

A full-time working mother should be able to support her family at the current minimum wage, yet even two full-time working parents often struggle. The minimum wage must be raised. We must do this not only because we value our workers and want to compensate them accordingly (and help them avoid needing subsidies and/or welfare to live), but also because we recognize that parents across America need sufficient income to raise healthy children who become productive, gainfully employed adults.

Something is clearly amiss when the federal minimum wage is completely insufficient for basic subsistence. This is an issue that affects all Americans, but it's particularly important for women, who still earn less than men for the same work, and even more so for working mothers, who earn less than women without children. Mothers need to be paid fairly. This means equal pay for equal work, and a minimum wage that provides full-time workers with a basic livelihood.

Chapter "R"—Realistic and Fair Wages

Mothers need to be able to support their families. Equal pay should be given for equal work. Full-time jobs that pay wages so low that parents must use public programs to feed, house, or look after the medical needs of their children are not the kind of jobs that are good for America. A strong economy requires jobs that pay a living wage.

Action: Mothers want—

(1)   A minimum wage that is a living wage.

(2)   Equal pay for equal work.

To make a difference, go to **www.MotherhoodManifesto.com**.

8

As Mothers Go, So Goes the Country

Lorri pulled the baby bottle out of her briefcase and smiled. It had been a tough morning. A mother of two, Lorri woke up around 5 A.M. to the sound of the phone ringing. It was her childcare provider calling to say she was too sick to watch children that day.

The marathon began. Her children, aged six months and two years, were still in bed. That quickly changed as Lorri and her husband raced to get them to her job-sponsored "back-up day-care." Adding to Lorri's stress was the fact that she had an important meeting scheduled for 7:30 A.M.

They all got in the car, commuting as a family since her husband's work was just a few blocks from her own. First stop was the Juice Joint, her husband's restaurant, where the family breakfasted on spicy egg wraps, cereal, and, of course, juice.

Lorri called the back-up daycare center from the restaurant to make sure there was space for the kids. Thankfully, space was available, and Lorri breathed a sigh of relief.

Professionally dressed, with a backpack on her back for the two-year-old's diapers, snacks, extra clothes, wipes, one toy, and blankie—all labeled at 6 A.M. with brown masking tape— and another bag for the baby on her arm, Lorri pushed an outdated 50-lb stroller down Fifteenth Street in Washington, D.C. "It was so hard balancing all the stuff, the backpack, the bag, the babies in the stroller with my briefcase in the basket under the stroller," recalls Lorri.

The kids, wired from the change in routine and the unfamiliar sounds of D.C. rush hour traffic, kept dropping things from the stroller as Lorri pushed them along. She picked the items up and stuffed them in any available spot as they rolled down the sidewalk.

The drop-in daycare opened at 7:30 A.M., the exact time Lorri was supposed to be at work, so she rushed to fill out the requisite forms and organize their food, toys, bottles, and blankies.

Ten blocks of speed-walking back to work brought a film of sweat to her body. Her pantsuit rumpled, she entered the conference room where her meeting was about to begin, opened her briefcase to take out the meeting materials, and found a leaking baby bottle, a bag of halved grapes, and random cheerios mixed in with her agenda.

One of the secretaries asked, "Did you forget something? Is there a baby here?" And Lorri broke the ice with her laughter.

By providing back-up daycare for children at $15 per child per day, Lorri's company ensured she was able make it to work on this particular day in early September and do her job well. She was able to maintain a high level of work productivity, and, quite importantly, didn't miss her meeting with several new hires. Without the company program, Lorri would likely have missed an important work day.

In the end, Lorri notes, "When you are a working mom, you really have to learn to laugh at yourself." Being a mother has made her "more organized at work and better at time management. . . . You really have to use time more efficiently after children, I don't know how you'd survive if you didn't."

Lorri is one example of how changes in workplace policies can increase worker productivity—improving a company's bottom line while providing a structure of support for families. Another company, Google, one of America's fastest-growing companies, has also taken steps to keep valuable employees in their workforce as they raise families. Google offers employees with children three months maternity leave at 75 percent pay, two weeks of free meals on wheels to new parents' homes, two weeks off with full pay for fathers, comfortable breast pumping rooms and a lactation program with free lactation consulting, special parking spaces for expectant mothers, childcare centers, healthcare coverage for the family, up to $5,000 per year for adoption assistance, and flexible work options.

Why go to all the effort? Stacy Sullivan, Director of Human Resources at Google, comments, "The goal has always been to create an amazing search engine to get information out into the world, and also to make this an incredible place to work for employees—a company where people really want to come every day, and a company that helps people take care of worries and stress at home so employees can be happy and more productive at work." This effort is paying off.

One employee, Ninette, a real estate planning manager, started about six years ago at the company. Her daughter, now two years old, stays in the Kinderplex—Google's workplace childcare facility—and is learning gymnastics, dance, preschool cur- riculum, and art while her mom works in her office, which is about five minutes away. The transition to working mother has been easy for Ninette—after having her daughter, she took three months off with 75 percent pay and came back to work part-time for a few weeks; then she later transitioned to a four-day work week until her daughter was older. Ninette kept her job at Google as her daughter grew into the cute little person she is today, prac- ticing "Jingle Bells" for her preschool holiday show in the car, on the phone with her grandmother and aunts, and at other times only a two-year-old would think to belt out a holiday tune long after the season is over. "She really enjoys it, and it's cool to see her taking these things home with her," comments Ninette.

Ninette continues, sharing her feelings about the Kinderplex as well as support she's received from Google, "It's been a godsend for me. I drop her off, and once I'm gone she has a great time. I don't worry about her while I'm at work, and it's pretty flexible because the company has always stressed work/life balance from the top. If you ever have to leave early, it's understandable." The company was able to keep a terrific real estate planning manager, and Ninette was able to balance her job with her growing family. It's a win/win situation.

Moving Forward

Not all companies are able to provide this much family support. In fact, most can't. However, a combination of government and business initiatives could provide this much support for all types of jobs. The cost of paid family leave for new parents needs to be an expense our society shares as we recognize the value of providing parents with what they need to raise healthy children. Offering flexibility in work hours is an opportunity many companies can embrace without hurting the bottom line (and often actually helping it). The cost of healthcare for individuals, let alone families, has risen to the point where our economy is suffering— a joint effort by government and business working together to improve our healthcare system is long overdue. Lorri and Ninette's experiences show it's possible to better balance work and family. We need to make basic supports available to all parents.

In order to do so, we first have to face the fact that times have changed and most modern families have two working parents. This is not inherently a problem if we, as a country, embrace both the need to work and the need to care for family. But to truly embrace both work and family, changes have to be made.

It's time to start thinking outside the box. We have to face up to the fact that the status quo is not adequate for most working mothers, and that in most cases there are not enough incentives for businesses to take up the slack. This is leading to a situation that is increasingly untenable for working mothers and their children.

FEMINISTS ARE MOTHERS, TOO

by Kim Gandy, President, National Organization for Women (NOW)

There was a titter as the women looked to their interpreter to see if I was joking. They were from countries not known for women's advances (Jordan, Saudi Arabia, Qatar) and found it hard to believe U.S. family leave policies were so inferior to their own. But it's true. Unlike most of the world, our country treats child-rearing as each family's private burden, rather than a societal priority.

Our politicians talk about "family values," but do little that values families.

For nearly forty years, NOW has worked toward equal rights, broader opportunities, and respect for women—in all the work we do. After all, we coined the rallying cry: "Every Mother is a Working Mother."

But we have a long way to go until most women (and men) have genuine choices, freely made . . . until caregivers are given both respect and financial security . . . until people stop saying "women can't have it all" and start asking "why are women expected to do it all."

It's time to start working toward national solutions to support parent-friendly working environments. Taking good care of family and being an exemplary employee does not need to be an either/or choice. We can do both. Changes in public policy, along with cultural and policy changes within companies, will help working mothers while improving our collective economic bottom line. From company-sponsored back-up childcare to universal healthcare for all children, from paid family leave to flexible work options, the solutions are out there.

These are not merely ideals we aspire to, but concrete national

NOW has consistently sought economic recognition and financial security for mothers and caregivers—like our Homemaker's Bill of Rights legislation. But creating a genuine work-life balance would mean long-sought changes in our country and culture. It would mean achieving what we've demanded for forty years: paid family leave, universal high-quality childcare and healthcare, support for poor mothers, full reproductive options, real job flexibility—and fathers doing their fair share. Just for starters.

Our progress thus far (job protection for pregnant women, unpaid family leave, childcare deductions, awareness of work/family conflict) is a direct result of concerted action by the feminist movement, despite strong resistance to changing the status quo. But there is much more to do. Our NOW Committee on Mothers and Caregivers' Economic Rights is helping chapters form grassroots taskforces across the country to expand women's choices. Both women and children, and yes, even men, will benefit.

Kim Gandy has been active in NOW for thirty-two years and was elected President in 2001. She is an attorney and lives in Silver Spring, Maryland, with her partner, Kip Lornell, and their two pre-teen daughters.

policies: policies that will help our economy by ensuring mothers are able to contribute to their full potential; policies that will help our communities by ensuring children have the support they need to be healthy; and most of all policies that will help children by allowing them to grow up in homes that are able to support and nurture them in order to allow them the opportunity that should be the right of every American—the opportunity to succeed in life.

- **M** = Maternity/Paternity Leave: Paid family leave for all parents after a new child comes into the family.
- **O** = Open Flexible Work: Give parents the ability to structure their work hours and careers in a way that allows them to meet both business and family needs. This includes flexible work hours and locations, part-time work options, as well as the ability to move in and out of the labor force to raise young children without penalties.
- **T** = TV We Choose and Other After School Programs: Give families safe, educational opportunities for children after the school doors close for the day, including: Create a clear and independent universal television rating system for parents, with technology that allows them to choose what is showing in their own homes; support quality educational programming for kids; increase access to, and funding, for after-school programs.
- **H** = Healthcare for All Kids: Provide quality, universal healthcare to all children.

- **E** = Excellent Childcare: Quality, affordable childcare should be available to all parents who need it. Childcare providers should be paid at least a living wage and healthcare benefits.
- **R** = Realistic and Fair Wages: Two full-time working parents should be able to earn enough to adequately care for their family. In addition, working mothers must receive equal pay for equal work.

The Motherhood Manifesto highlights shared needs of mothers and families across economic and social boundaries. There is a growing understanding that mothers need to be able to work *and* raise children. Paid family leave, flexible work structures, after-school programs, family health, childcare, and economic sufficiency are all important ways to support parent's efforts to care for their children. Any one Manifesto Point standing alone, unsupported by the others, is not sufficient. The Manifesto Points are all interconnected, creating a web of safety for families. That said, improvement in any one of these parts of our lives creates consequences that reverberate throughout. There is a convergence of need and opportunity when these issues are worked on together.

We all want children to grow up in a healthy environment that encourages them to develop to their full potential. Though we have achieved this for some families, many families still have to make choices that are too much like King Solomon's dilemma: No parent should have to choose between being able to care for their child and being able to feed their child; no parent should be put in a position where their income is less than their childcare costs; no parent should be forced into a job merely to keep their healthcare coverage; and most of all, no woman should be punished economically with lower wages and less chance for advancement because she chose to start a family.

Nurturing children requires us to take the long view. In a culture where short-term profits and losses are often the tipping point for decisions, we have to think decades out into the future. This is a stretch for some companies that haven't been around for more than a decade, and also for some politicians who just want to get re-elected next year. Yet more and more parents find they've acquired a long view when they look into the faces of their sons and daughters. These parents realize that when we take a short-term approach at the expense of long-term benefits, we are really taking from our children. Our children are depending on us to provide them with a mother who is not discriminated against at work, to provide them with the wherewithal to get to a doctor when they are sick, to allow them the right to be children and not grow up in a environment that is saturated with themes and ideas suitable only for adults, and to allow them to live in a home that is able to provide for their basic needs.

It is our turn to act. There is a rising tide of consciousness that change is needed.

Taking Action

After a very rough time landing her first job in Pennsylvania, Kiki—whose story was shared in Chapter One—has been fully employed for over a decade. Her children are now grown and she is terribly proud of them. As a single mother with a full-time job it would have been easy, and vastly more comfortable, for her to forget the humiliation of ending up on welfare, but she didn't. She never wants her daughter to suffer the same discrimination that left her unemployed and dependent on government subsidies and food stamps.

So Kiki has been working with the nonprofit organization, 9 to 5 National Association of Working Women, for over a decade advocating that Pennsylvania pass a law to protect single mothers like her from bias in hiring. They haven't succeeded yet—and neither have people in more than half of the states in our nation, which also leave mothers unprotected from discrimination based on their marital/familial status during job discussions.[1] This problem is bigger than Pennsylvania.

Kiki hasn't given up. October 2005 marked the fiftieth anniversary of the Pennsylvania Human Relations Act legislation that Kiki is working to amend so mothers can't be asked questions about their marital and childbearing status in job interviews.

This particular amendment has been stuck in a legislative committee for the past three legislative sessions. To commemorate the Golden Anniversary date, as well as to draw attention to the languishing amendment, Kiki went to a local party store after work one day and purchased stationary decorated with golden balloons and ribbons. She then brought her new purchase back to the home office she shares with her cat, Eddie, and went to work.

THE MOTHERS' MOVEMENT

by Judith Stadtman Tucker, Editor, the Mothers Movement Online

Just as we now look back at events that set earlier waves of the women's rights movement in motion, perhaps the first quarter of the twenty-first century will be remembered as a period of renewed outrage over the persistent relationship between motherhood and women's inequality.

Today, the nation's mothers are calling for change—in popular books describing the nature and origins of the contemporary motherhood problem, through formal advocacy statements issued by mothers' support groups, and in the emerging public forum of a progressive-alternative mothers' media.

The new breed of outspoken mothers is perfectly clear about what they want. They want mothers and fathers to have more and better

Kiki's home office is sparsely decorated with oak furniture, a purple rug, and the electronic devices needed to for advocacy: computer, fax, scanner, and printer. Copies of the state house and senate amendments are carefully tacked on her bulletin board along with prized pictures of her daughter's college graduation and her son's wedding. And a special place is reserved for the card she got from her daughter with a picture of Rosie the Riveter that says, "We Can Do It."

In this office, surrounded by oak bookcases filled with papers, letters, and over a decade of advocacy history on this legislation; and comfortably situated in her favorite yard sale find, a purple secretary's chair, Kiki drafted the text for the golden stationary that she would mail to all the state legislators in Pennsylvania: "You are cordially invited to end discrimination against Pennsylvanians in the job hiring process. October 27, 2005, marks the 50th Anniversary of options for integrating work and family life. They want respect and recognition for the social and economic value of mothers' work—both paid employment and the unpaid caring work mothers do at home. They want flexible workplaces, more control over working hours, and equal pay for equal work. They want to close the critical gaps in U.S. family policy, and they want reasonable protection from economic hardship they may incur due to their maternal status. Above all, mothers' advocates view the need for these adjustments as a social justice issue, and are working to mobilize an organized social movement—a diverse grassroots uprising—to move their concerns to the forefront of the national agenda.

The mothers' movement, while still in its infancy, is rapidly gaining momentum. Across America and around the world, mothers—and others—who think about social change are ready to act.

the enactment of the Pennsylvania Human Relations Act." The letter goes on to describe history of the bill and the last line says, "On this Golden Anniversary of this Act, I cordially invite you to please vote *YES* to eliminate discrimination against the people of Pennsylvania based on their marital/familial status. Please vote *YES* when this bill comes before your committee for a vote and please vote *YES* when the bills are passed on to the floor for a vote."

Kiki recalls, "To make it look like a party invitation I put an RSVP with my phone number at the bottom. I received a total of six phone calls; one of which was an aide to say her boss could not attend. I said, 'Well, if you read it carefully, then you would see that it's not a party, it's a request for help." Kiki then asked the aide to please read it again and ask her boss for help. The other calls Kiki received from legislators were all favorable, but the amendment still didn't move forward.

The fight continues, and while Kiki keeps advocating for the amendment to move out of committee with the help of organizations like 9to5 and the Pennsylvania Commission for Women (a state commission enacted by the governor), she's been gathering together with friends to knit scarves for mothers who are visiting food pantries.

"We get hammered with 'Toys for tots, toys for tots!' but moms are left out," comments Kiki. "These scarves are going to be infused with love for women we don't know, but who are just like I was. I figure that if I can't stop the job discrimination right now, then at least I'll knit some scarves to keep them warm." Kiki thinks for a moment and then says, "But why not give the gift that will last all year which is dignity, and do this by getting involved in politics and putting pressure on the legislators to make anti-descrimination bills a reality?"

Kiki's encountered more than a few people who are astonished to hear her story, "Many people can't even fathom that we live in a society that is so cold and callous against mothers that they are deterred from getting jobs simply because they have children. But just because it isn't happening to you, doesn't mean it isn't happening. And that's the truth of it. When people start talking about these issues and realizing how backwards we can be in terms of keeping up with the times, then changes will happen."

There are women, men, and parents like Kiki working on important family issues across our nation. Just like Kiki, all need our help and support to move these issues forward. By coming together we can help make the changes necessary to level the playing field and support America families.

America can design work to be compatible with good parenting, and we can provide needed resources for working parents. Our country will be stronger as a consequence. Society needs kids—we all depend on a vibrant younger generation to take care of us. Many of the visibly explosive issues of the day—retirement security, Medicare, exploding health costs—are symptoms of a society that is aging. We can fuss over the numbers all day long, but in the end nothing works if we don't raise children to take the world forward when we're ready to retire. The economic strength of our country relies on healthy families.

In the last few years there has been a rapidly growing awareness of the need for meaningful support for parents and children. However there is a remarkable quiet in the halls of power on these issues. Legislation for paid family leave, paid sick leave, childcare, and benefits for part-time work has been introduced. But this legislation has remained stuck in committees and largely invisible to the average citizen. It is time for millions of citizens to work together and empower leaders with vision. Citizens can and must initiate change in their local and national communities.

Aided by emerging internet activism, political engagement has grown dramatically in the last decade. MoveOn.org, cofounded by one of this book's authors, is an example of how citizens working together can make a difference. With MoveOn, friends tell friends about ways they can engage, and now MoveOn has well over three million members who amplify each other's voices. These members have helped define the advocacy agenda for the organization, created amazing ads, hosted press events across the nation, delivered petitions to senators in every state, made millions of phone calls, provided political backing to good leaders, effectively opposed some very bad policies, and raised millions of dollars in small contributions for candidates who reflect their values. And after Hurricane Katrina, tens of thousands of MoveOn members opened their homes to hurricane victims. The hearts of Americans are big, and this is why a movement to ensure mothers and families are supported is ultimately going to be successful.

This type of organizing, and more, can be done to provide paid family leave, open flexible workplaces, after school programs, healthcare for all children, excellent childcare, as well as realistic and fair wages. The opportunities for constructive change are vast.

The time has come to begin a new discussion about motherhood in America, to join together to create a groundswell of support for change, to tell elected leaders our priorities, to make the issues facing mothers central to our policy discussions, to solve these problems—because nothing is more important to the continued success of our nation than guaranteeing the health and happiness of our greatest and most important investment, our children.

To make change, go to **www.MotherhoodManifesto.com**.

Readers Guide

1. How do the issues covered in the *Motherhood Manifesto* affect your family? *As a refresher, the core issues covered are: Maternity/ paternity leave—paid family leave; Open flexible work options; TV and other after school programs; Healthcare for all children; Excellent childcare; and Realistic and fair wages.*

2. Which motherhood issues impact your family the most?

3. What would your top three points be if you were writing a Motherhood Manifesto?

4. This book argues that many of the personal family issues faced by Americans (like struggling with unpaid leave, childcare, and healthcare) are really issues that we have to take on as a society. It argues that when so many families are struggling with the same issues, then these struggles are an indicator of a structural problem, not personal failings. What do you think?

5. The United States is one of only two industrialized countries that do not offer paid maternity leave to working women (163 countries give women paid leave with the birth of a child). How much should international standards and programs inform American standards and programs?

6. Open flexible work is good for parents and workers in general. Do you think it is good for business? In what ways is it

good and in what ways is it bad? Would flexible work options be useful in your workplace?

7. Now that most children's parents work, most children don't have parents to go home to after school. What programs should be available to kids after school?

8. Is the current healthcare system working for you and your loved ones at this time? What do you like about it? What would you want to improve?

9. Some states are implementing pre-kindergarten education to ensure young children are ready for school when they start. Would you support this in your state?

10. Were you aware that there is a substantial gap between what women who are mothers and women who aren't mothers are paid? Do you think broader understanding of this statistic would mobilize citizens and leaders to provide mothers with more economic protections, including family-friendly programs?

11. What action to support mothers/parents do you think has the most potential at this time?

To join an online dialogue about these issues, log on to the **www.MotherhoodManifesto.com website.**

Notes

1. MOTHERHOOD IN AMERICA ENDNOTES:

1. Bureau of Labor Statistics, "Employed Persons by Occupation, Sex and Age," 2003-2004, Table 9, Page 207, www.bls.gov/cps/cpsaat9.pdf (accessed January 2006).

2. New America Foundation, "New America Foundation Proposes Bold Workplace Flexibility Policy for All Working Parents and Releases Data Showing Families Running Harder to Stay in Place," news release, June 23, 2005, www.newamerica.net/Download_Docs/pdfs/Doc_File_2438_1.pdf.

3. American women now make up 47 percent of the entire paid labor force. Women aged twenty-five to thirty-four have seen a dramatic rise in labor. force participation, from 63 percent in 1975 to a much higher 81 percent in 1999. A full 72 percent of American mothers work outside of the home. Bureau of Labor Statistics, "Employed Persons by Occupation, Sex and Age"; Deirdre Gaquin, *Special Tabulations of the March 1975 and March 2000 Current Population Surveys* (Women's Research and Education Institute, 2001), in Cynthia B. Costello et al., *The American Woman 2003–2004: Daughters of a Revolution—Young Women Today* (New York: Palgrave Macmillan, 2003), 62; and Barbara Downs, *Fertility of American Women: June 2002,* Current Population Reports, U.S. Census Bureau, Washington, D.C., 2003, www.census.gov/prod/2003pubs/p20-548.pdf.

4. Downs, *Fertility of American Women: June 2002.*

5. In 1980, mothers earned 56 percent of men's salaries, while non-mothers earned 66 percent (a 10 percent mommy wage gap). But by 1991, non-mothers' earnings rocketed to 90.1 percent, while mothers earned only 72.6 percent (an increased 17.5 percent mommy wage gap). SOURCE: Jane Waldfogel, "Understanding the 'Family Gap' in Pay for Women with Children," *Journal of Economic Perspectives* 12, no. 1 (1998): 137–156.

6. Jane Waldfogel, "Understanding the 'Family Gap' in Pay for Women with Children," *Journal of Economic Perspectives* 12, no. 1 (1998), 137–156.

7. U.S. Census Bureau, "People: Income and Employment," 2005, http://factfinder.census.gov/jsp/saff/SAFFInfo.jsp?_pageId=tp6_income_employment.

8. Waldfogel, "Understanding the 'Family Gap.'"

9. Children's Defense Fund calculations, based on data from the U.S. Census Bureau, Current Population Survey Annual Demographic Supplement,

Detailed Income Tables, "Table FINC-03. Presence of Related Children Under 18 Years Old—All Families, by Total Money Income in 2001, Type of Family Work Experience in 2001, Race and Hispanic Origin of Reference Person," ferret.bls.census.gov/macro/032002/faminc/new03_000.htm.

10. USDA Food and Nutrition Service, "Fact Sheet on Resources, Income, and Benefits," October 2005, www.fns.usda.gov/fsp/applicant_recipients/fs_Res_Ben_Elig.htm.

11. Shelley Correll, "Getting a Job: Is There a Motherhood Penalty?" (paper presented at the American Sociological Association's 100th annual meeting in Philadelphia, PA, August 15, 2005); Daniel Aloi, "Mothers Face Disadvantages in Getting Hired, Cornell Study Says," Cornell University News Service, August 4, 2005, www.news.cornell.edu/stories/Aug05/soc.mothers.dea.html

12. Jyoti Thottam, "Reworking Work," *Time,* July 25, 2005, www.time.com/time/archive/preview/0,10987,1083900,00.html; James T. Bond et al., *2005 National Study of Employers: Highlights of Findings* (Families and Work Institute, 2005), familiesandwork.org/summary/2005nsesummary.pdf; and Families and Work Institute, "*2005 National Study of Employers* Reveals Changes in Work Life Assistance Offered to America's Employees," news release, October 13, 2005, familiesandwork.org/press/2005nserelease.html#nse.

13. Bond et al., *2005 National Study*; and Families and Work Institute, "*2005 National Study of Employers* Reveals Changes."

14. U.S. Census Bureau, "Table H1: Percent Childless and Births per 1,000 Women in the Last Year: Selected Years, 1976 to Present," October 23, 2003, www.census.gov/population/socdemo/fertility/tabH1.pdf.

15. xvi. Gaquin, *Special Tabulations.* in Costello et al., *The American Woman 2003–2004,* 62.

16. Waldfogel, "Understanding the 'Family Gap.' "

17. U.S. Census Bureau, "People: Income and Employment."

18. Sylvia Ann Hewlett and Carolyn Buck Luce, "Off Ramps and On-Ramps: Keeping Talented Women on the Road to Success," *Harvard Business Review,* March 2005.

2. Maternity/Paternity Leave Endnotes:

1. Bureau of Labor Statistics, "Employment Characteristics of Families Summary," news release, June 9, 2005, www.bls.gov/news.release/famee.nr0.htm.

2. Jodi Grant et al., *Expecting Better: A State-by-State Analysis of Parental Leave Programs* (Washington, D.C.: National Partnership for Women and Families,

2005), www.nationalpartnership.org/portals/p3/library/PaidLeave/Parental-LeaveReportMay05.pdf, 48–49.

3. Jody Heymann et al., *The Work, Family, and Equity Index: Where Does the United States Stand Globally?* (Boston: Project on Global Working Families, 2004), www.hsph.harvard.edu/globalworkingfamilies/images/report.pdf.

4. Ibid.

5. Ibid.

6. Human Resources and Skills Development Canada, "Employment Insurance (EI) and Maternity, Parental and Sickness Benefits," www.hrsdc.gc.ca/asp/gateway.asp?hr=en/ei/types/special.shtml&hs=tyt#Maternity3.

7. In Sweden, according to the European Industrial Relations Observatory (EIRO), "Parental leave runs for 480 days, of which 390 days are paid at the same rate as for sick pay—i.e. 80 percent of normal pay (up to a ceiling). Parents each have a legal right to take 50 percent of the leave, but one parent can transfer some of their entitlement to the other. However, 60 days of the leave may not be transferred. This part of the leave is called the 'mother months' and 'father months' respectively." Annika Berg, "Commission to Examine Parental Leave," European Industrial Relations Observatory Online, www.eiro.eurofound.eu.int/2004/06/inbrief/se0406102n.html.

8. Ann Crittenden, *The Price of Motherhood: Why the Most Important Job in the World Is Still the Least Valued* (Henry Holt and Company, 2002), 248.

9. Grant et al., *Expecting Better*, 7.

10. Ibid., 6.

11. Christopher J. Ruhm, "Parental Leave and Child Health" (working paper, National Bureau of Economic Research, Cambridge, MA, May 1998), www.nber.org/papers/w6554.

12. Kristin Smith et al., *Maternity Leave and Employment Patterns: 1961–1995*, Current Population Reports, U.S. Census Bureau, Washington, D.C., 2001, www.census.gov/prod/2001pubs/p70-79.pdf.

13. Barbara Downs, *Fertility of American Women: June 2002*, Current Population Reports, U.S. Census Bureau, Washington, D.C., 2003, www.census.gov/prod/2003pubs/p20-548.pdf.

14. Ruhm, "Parental Leave and Child Health."

15. Heymann et al., *The Work, Family, and Equity Index*, 7–8.

16. World Health Organization, *The World Health Report 2005: Make Every Mother and Child Count*, 182–185, www.who.int/whr/2005/annex/annexe2a_en.pdf.

17. Emily Fenichel et al., *Partnerships for Quality: Improving Infant-Toddler child-care for Low-Income Families* (Princeton, NJ: Mathematica Policy Research, Inc., 2002), www.mathematica-mpr.com/pdfs/partnership.pdf.

18. Susanna Loeb et al., "childcare in Poor Communities: Early Learning Effects of Type, Quality, and Stability," *Child Development* 75, no. 1 (2004), pace.berkeley.edu/Stanford_Child_Dev_Findings.pdf.

19. Grant et al., *Expecting Better,* 8.

20. Grant et al., *Expecting Better,* 9.

21. Jane Waldfogel, "Family and Medical Leave: Evidence from the 2000 Surveys," *Monthly Labor Review* 124, no. 9 (September 2001), 17–23.

22. Sakiko Tanaka, "Parental Leave and Child Health Across OECD Countries," *Economic Journal* 115, no. 501 (2005), 7–28.

23. Grant et al., *Expecting Better.*

24. Ibid., 7.

25. Heymann et al., *The Work, Family, and Equity Index,* 8.

26. Smith et al., *Maternity Leave and Employment Patterns.* Also see Katherin Ross Phillips, *Getting Time Off: Access to Leave Among Working Parents* (Washington, D.C.: Urban Institute, 2004), www.urban.org/UploadedPDF/310977_B-57.pdf.

27. Grant et al., *Expecting Better,* 8.

3. FLEXIBLE WORK ENDNOTES:

1. Sylvia Ann Hewlett and Carolyn Buck Luce, "Off-Ramps and On-Ramps: Keeping Talented Women on the Road to Success," *Harvard Business Review,* March 1, 2005, 8–9.

2. According to the AFL-CIO, "One study found that flextime is available to nearly two-thirds (62 percent) of workers of more than $71,000 a year but to less than one-third (31 percent) of working parents with incomes less than $28,000." American Federation of Labor and Congress of Industrial Organizations, "Family Friendly Work Schedules," www.aflcio.org/issues/workfamily/workschedules.cfm.

3. Martin H. Malin et al., *Work/Family Conflict, Union Style: Labor Arbitrations Involving Family Care* (Washington, D.C.: Program on WorkLife Law, 2004), 9. This story also appears in Miriam Peskowitz, *The Truth Behind the Mommy Wars: Who Decides What Makes a Good Mother?* (Emeryville, CA: Seal Press, 2005), 123–124.

4. Malin et al., *Work/Family Conflict, Union Style,* 9.

5. Ibid.

6. AFL-CIO, "Family Friendly Work Schedules."

7. Hewlett and Buck Luce, "Off-Ramps and On-Ramps," 5.

8. Ibid.

9. Joyce P. Jacobsen and Laurence M. Levin, "The Effects of Intermittent Labor Force Attachment on Women's Earnings," *Monthly Labor Review* 118, no. 9 (September 1995), www.bls.gov/opub/mlr/1995/09/art2full.pdf.

10. Families and Work Institute, "*2005 National Study of Employers* Reveals Changes in Work Life Assistance Offered to America's Employees," news release, October 13, 2005, familiesandwork.org/press/2005nserelease.html; and Rhona Rapoport et al., *Beyond Work-Family Balance: Advancing Gender Equity and Workplace Performance* (San Francisco: Jossey-Bass, 2002).

11. Hewlett and Buck Luce, "Off-Ramps and On-Ramps."

12. Ibid, 1.

13. Lotte Bailyn et al., "Unexpected Connections: Considering Employees' Personal Lives Can Revitalize Your Business," *MIT Sloan Management Review* 38, no. 4 (Summer 1997), 11–19; and Rapoport et al., *Beyond Work-Family Balance,* 67–68.

14. Jyoti Thottam, "Reworking Work," *Time,* July 25, 2005, www.time.com/time/archive/preview/0,10987,1083900,00.html.

15. Ibid.

16. Hewlett and Buck Luce, "Off-Ramps and On-Ramps," 9.

17. Thottam, "Reworking Work."

18. Families and Work Institute, "*2005 National Study of Employers* Reveals Changes."

19. Ibid.

20. James T. Bond et al., *When Work Works: Summary of Families and Work Institute Research Findings,* Families and Work Institute, familiesandwork.org/3w/research/downloads/3wes.pdf.

21. Ibid.

22. Karen Kornbluh, *Win-Win Flexibility* (Washington, D.C.: New America Foundation, 2005), www.newamerica.net/Download_Docs/pdfs/Doc_File_2436_1.pdf.

23. "Employed, married women with household before tax income levels ranging from $10,000 to $74,999 have decreased odds of using flextime compared with those having household incomes of $75,000 and above." Jodi R. Billings

and Deanna L. Sharpe, "Factors Influencing Flextime Usage Among Employed Married Women," *Consumer Interests Annual* 45 (1999), 92.

24. Carol Ostrom, "Jobs to Share," in John de Graaf, ed., *Take Back Your Time: Fighting Overwork and Time Poverty in America* (San Francisco: Berrett-Koehler Publishers, 2003), 146–153.

25. "Part-time professionals reported less work-to-family conflict in terms of interference and strain than full-time professional (2.4, and 3.0 on a scale from 1-5)." "Part-Time Work: Work-to-Family Conflict," Sloan Work and Family Research Network, wfnetwork.bc.edu/statistics_template .php?id=1704&topic=10, from E. Jeffrey Hill et al., "New-Concept Part-Time Employment as a Work-Family Adaptive Strategy for Women Professionals with Small Children," *Family Relations* 53, no. 3 (2004), 282–292. Also see Sloan Work and Family Research Network, "Part-Time Work," wfnetwork.bc.edu/topic_extended.php?id=10&type=1.

26. "Among full- and part-time employees who work for organizations that employ part-time workers, 61 percent say that part-timers receive less than pro rata pay and benefits compared with full-time employees in the same positions just because they work part-time." Sloan Work and Family Research Network, "Part-Time Work: Less Benefits than Full-Time Work in the Same Position," wfnetwork.bc.edu/statistics_template.php?id= 1728&topic=10, from the National Study of the Changing Workforce, Families and Work Institute, 2002.

27. "In 2001, 18.5 percent of regular part-time workers had health insurance coverage provided by their employer, [compared to] 69 percent of regular full-time employees." Sloan Work and Family Research Network, "Health Insurance Coverage Lower for Part-Time Workers than Full-Time Workers," wfnetwork.bc.edu/statistics_template.php?id=1718&topic=10, from Jeffrey Wenger, *Share of Workers in "Nonstandard" Jobs Declines* (Washington, D.C.: Economic Policy Institute, 2003).

28. "According to a study of municipal employers, 'There are significantly less benefits provided to part-time workers as opposed to full-time workers. Part-time employees are covered for the following: vacation (44 percent), sick leave (18 percent), pension (34 percent), health insurance (21 percent), life insurance (18 percent), dental insurance (16 percent). More full-time employees are covered for the same benefits: vacation (95 percent), sick leave (56 percent), pension (79 percent), health insurance (76 percent), life insurance (87 percent), dental insurance (59 percent).'" "Part-time employees covered for less benefits than full-time employees," Sloan Work and Family

Research Network, wfnetwork.bc.edu/statistics_template.php?id=1736 &topic=10, from Gary E. Roberts, "Municipal Government Part-Time Employee Benefits Practices," *Public Personnel Management* 32, no. 3 (2003), 435–454.

29. "The Center for WorkLife Law," Word document e-mailed to author, September 2005.

30. Rapoport et al., *Beyond Work-Family Balance,* 67–68.

31. Joan Williams, *Unbending Gender: Why Family and Work Conflict and What to Do About It* (New York: Oxford University Press, 2000), 89–90.

32. Ariane Hegewisch et al., *Working Time for Working Families: Europe and the United States* (Washington, D.C.: Friedrich-Ebert-Stiftung, 2005), www.uchastings.edu/site_files/WLL/FESWorkingTimePublication.pdf, 55.

33. Ibid., 69.

34. National Association of childcare Resource and Referral Agencies, *childcare in America,* www.naccrra.org/docs/Child_Care_In_America_Facts.pdf; and Eugene Smolensky and Jennifer Appleton Gootman, eds., *Working Families and Growing Kids: Caring for Children and Adolescents* (Washington, D.C.: National Academies Press: 2003), www.nap.edu/openbook/0309087031/html/43.html.

35. NACCRRA, *childcare in America*; Smolensky and Appleton Gootman, *Working Families and Growing Kids*; U.S. Census Bureau, "Women's History Month, March 1–31," press release, February 14, 2003, www.census.gov/Press-Release/www/2003/cb03ff03.html; and U.S. Census Bureau, "Labor Force Participation for Mothers with Infants Declines for First Time, Census Bureau Reports," press release, October 18, 2001, www.census.gov/Press-Release/www/2001/cb01-170.html.

36. Barbara Downs, *Fertility of American Women: June 2002,* Current Population Reports, U.S. Census Bureau, Washington, D.C., 2003. This paragraph originally appeared in Kristin Rowe-Finkbeiner, *The F-Word: Feminism in Jeopardy* (Emeryville, CA: Seal Press, 2004).

37. Downs, *Fertility of American Women.*

38. Donald Hernandez, *We the American . . . Children,* U.S. Census Bureau, Washington, D.C., 1993, www.census.gov/apsd/wepeople/we-10.pdf.

39. Jodi Grant et al., *Expecting Better: A State-by-State Analysis of Parental Leave Programs* (Washington, D.C.: National Partnership for Women and Families, 2005), www.nationalpartnership.org/portals/p3/library/PaidLeave/ParentalLeaveReportMay05.pdf, 7.

40. Jacobsen and Levin, "The Effects of Intermittent Labor Force Attachment."

41. Ibid.

42. Ibid.

43. Anne J. Stone and Jennifer E. Griffith, *Older Women: The Economics of Aging* (Washington, D.C.: Women's Research and Education Institute, 1998), 35.

44. This passage originally appeared in *The F-Word*.

45. This paragraph originally appeared in *The F-Word*.

46. Center for Women's Business Research, *A Compendium of National Statistics on Women-Owned Businesses in the U.S.,* report prepared for the National Women's Business Council, September 2001, www.nwbc.gov/documents/compendium.pdf.

47. Total leave is better in the thirty Organization for Economic Co-operation and Development (OECD) member countries. The OECD is an intergovernmental organization of industrialized countries. Anna Cristina d'Addio and Marco Mira d'Ercole, "Trends and Determinants of Fertility Rates in OECD Countries: The Role of Policies" (working paper, Organisation for Economic Co-operation and Development, Paris, November 2005), www.oecd.org/dataoecd/7/33/35304751.pdf, page 57.

48. Kornbluh, *Win-Win Flexibility,* 1.

49. Hewlett and Buck Luce, "Off-Ramps and On-Ramps," 11.

50. Sylvia Ann Hewlett et al., *The Hidden Brain Drain: Off-Ramps and On-Ramps in Women's Careers* (Harvard Business School Press, 2005).

51. Hewlett and Buck Luce, "Off-Ramps and On-Ramps," 4.

4. TV We Choose and Other After-School Programs Endnotes:

1. American Academy of Pediatrics, "Television: What Children See and Learn," www.aap.org/pubed/ZZZNKWJGQ2D.htm?&sub_cat=1.

2. Institute of Medicine, "Advertising, Marketing and the Media: Improving Messages," September 2004, www.iom.edu/Object.File/Master/22/609/0.pdf, drawn from Jeffrey P. Koplan et al., eds., *Preventing Childhood Obesity: Health in the Balance* (Washington, D.C.: National Academies Press, 2005).

3. The Center on Media and Child Health, "The Effects of Electronic Media on Children Ages Zero to Six: A History of Research," January 2005, Kaiser Family Foundation, www.kff.org/entmedia/upload/The-Effects-of-Electronic-Media-on-Children-Ages-Zero-to-Six-A-History-of-Research-Issue-Brief.pdf, 4.

4. Ibid., 4.

5. Ibid., 7 and 9.

6. Kaiser Family Foundation, " 'Media Multi-tasking' Changing the Amount and Nature of Young People's Media Use," news release, March 9, 2005, www.kff.org/entmedia/entmedia030905nr.cfm.

7. Ibid.

8. Craig A. Anderson et al., "The Influence of Media Violence on Youth," *Psychological Science in the Public Interest* 4, no. 3 (2003), www.psychologicalscience.org/pdf/pspi/pspi43.pdf; Kevin W. Saunders, "The V-Chip: Coming Up Short or Unconstitutional Overreaching?" *West Virginia Journal of Law and Technology* 1, no. 1 (1997), www.wvu.edu/~law/wvjolt/Arch/Saunde/Saunde.htm; and Common Sense Media, "Impact of Media," www.commonsensemedia.org/resources/index.php.

9. Todd Gitlin, "Is Media Violence Free Speech?" debate between George Gerbner and Todd Gitlin, HotWired, July 9, 1997, www.hotwired.com/synapse/braintennis/97/27/right2.html.

10. Eugene V. Beresin, MD, "Media Violence and Youth," *Academic Psychiatry* 23 (1999), ap.psychiatryonline.org/cgi/content/abstract/23/2/111. Beresin referred to the study Sumiko Iwao et al. "Japanese and U.S. media: Some cross-cultural insights into TV violence," *Journal of Communication* 31 (1981), 28–36. Also see Center for Media Literacy, "Media Violence: Japan vs. America," www.medialit.org/reading_room/article538.html.

11. George Gerbner, "Is Media Violence Free Speech?" www.hotwired.com/synapse/braintennis/97/27/left2.html.

12. Indiana University School of Medicine, "Media Violence Linked to Concentration, Self-Control," news release, June 9, 2005, www.medicine.indiana.edu/news_releases/viewRelease.php4?art=346&print=true. The Indiana University School of Medicine research was published in Vincent P. Mathews et al., "Media Violence Exposure and Frontal Lobe Activation Measured by Functional Magnetic Resonance Imaging in Aggressive and Nonaggressive Adolescents," *Journal of Computer Assisted Tomography* 29 (May/June 2005), 287–292.

13. Kaiser Family Foundation, "Number of Sexual Scenes on TV Nearly Double Since 1998," news release, November 9, 2005, www.kff.org/entmedia/entmedia110905nr.cfm.

14. Rebecca L. Collins, PhD, et al., "Watching Sex on Television Predicts Adolescent Initiation of Sexual Behavior," *Pediatrics* 114, no. 3 (2004), pediatrics.aappublications.org/cgi/content/full/114/3/e280?eaf#SEC2; and Common Sense Media, "Teens Who Watch Sex on TV Are Twice as Likely to Have Sex

Themselves," September 7, 2004, www.commonsensemedia.org/resources/ sex_and_dating.php?id=3.

15. Kaiser Family Foundation, " 'Media Multi-tasking' Changing the Amount and Nature of Young People's Media Use."

16. Ibid.

17. Federal Communications Commission, "How to Prevent Viewing Objection-able Television Programs," ftp.fcc.gov/cgb/consumerfacts/objectionable tv.html.

18. Federal Communications Commission, "The TV Parental Guidelines," www.fcc.gov/parents/parent_guide.html.

19. Kaiser Family Foundation, "Few Parents Use V-Chip to Block TV Sex and Vio-lence, But More Than Half Use TV Ratings to Pick What Kids Can Watch," news release, July 24, 2001, www.kff.org/entmedia/3158-V-Chip-release.cfm.

20. Ibid.

21. "MPAA System for Rating Films Offers Parents Little Guidance on Violent Content, Study Finds," *UCLA Public Health,* May 2005, www.ph.ucla.edu/ magazine/sph.6.05.research.pdf

22. Kaiser Family Foundation, "Few Parents Use V-Chip to Block TV Sex and Violence."

23. Federal Communications Commission, "TV Channel Blocking," www.fcc.gov/parents/channelblocking.html.

24. Karen Schulman, *Key Facts: Essential Information about childcare, Early Edu-cation and School-Age Care* (Children's Defense Fund, 2003), 5; and J. K. Posner and D. L. Vandell, "Low-Income Children's After-School Care: Are There Beneficial Effects of After-School Programs?" *Child Development* 65 (April 1994), www.ncbi.nlm.nih.gov/entrez/query.fcgi?cmd=Retrieve&db= PubMed&list_uids=8013233&dopt=Citation.

25. James Alan Fox, PhD, *Trends in Juvenile Violence: A Report to the United States Attorney General on Current and Future Rates of Juvenile Offending,* report prepared for the Bureau of Justice Statistics, United States Department of Justice, March 1996, www.ojp.usdoj.gov/bjs/pub/pdf/tjvfox2.pdf; and Fox, *Juvenile Violence in the After School Hours,* September 6, 1999, www.jfox.neu.edu/timeofday96web.htm.

26. Afterschool Alliance, *America After 3 PM: A Household Survey on Afterschool in America,* www.afterschoolalliance.org/press_archives/america_3pm/Executive_Summary.pdf.

27. William O. Brown et al., *The Costs and Benefits of After School Programs: The Estimated Effects of the After School Education and Safety Program Act of 2002,*

September 2002, rose.claremontmckenna.edu/publications/pdf/after_
school.pdf.

28. University of Otago, New Zealand, "Research Confirms Link Between TV
and Childhood Obesity," news release, September 13, 2005,
www.otago.ac.nz/news/news/2005/13-09-05_press_release.html.

5. HEALTHCARE FOR ALL KIDS ENDNOTES:

1. The Kaiser Family Foundation, "United States: Health Insurance Coverage of
Children 0–18," www.statehealthfacts.org/cgibin/healthfacts.cgi?action=
profile&area=United+States&category=Health+Coverage+%26+Unin-
sured&subcategory=Health+Insurance+Status&topic=Children+%280%2d
18%29.

2. David U. Himmelstein et al., "Illness and Injury as Contributors to Bankruptcy," *Health Affairs,* February 2, 2005, content.healthaffairs.
org/cgi/reprint/hlthaff.w5.63v1.

3. Ibid., W5-71.

4. Ibid., W5-63.

5. Ibid., W5-66.

6. Harvard Medical School, "Illness and Medical Bills Cause Half of All Bankruptcies," news release, February 2, 2005, www.hms.harvard.edu/
news/releases/2_2Himmelstein.html.

7. John Leland, "Insurance Is No Longer a Safeguard," *New York Times,* October
23, 2005.

8. Himmelstein et al., "Illness and Injury as Contributors to Bankruptcy," W5-70.

9. Harvard Medical School, "Illness and Medical Bills."

10. World Health Organization, *The World Health Report 2005: Make Every
Mother and Child Count,* www.who.int/whr/2005/annex/annexe6_en.pdf.

11. Ibid., www.who.int/whr/2005/annex/annexe1_en.pdf.

12. Ibid., www.who.int/whr/2005/annex/annexe2a_en.pdf.

13. Eileen R. Ellis et al., *Medicaid Enrollment in 50 States: December 2002 Update*
(Washington, D.C.: Kaiser Commission on Medicaid and the Uninsured,
2003), www.kff.org/medicaid/upload/Medicaid-Enrollment-in-50-States-
December-2002-Update.pdf.

14. Kaiser Commission on Medicaid and the Uninsured, *The Uninsured and Their
Access to healthcare* (Washington, D.C.: Kaiser Commission on Medicaid
and the Uninsured, 2005), www.kff.org/uninsured/upload/The-Uninsured-
and-Their-Access-to-Health-Care-Fact-Sheet-6.pdf.

15. Ibid.

16. Kaiser Commission, *Covering the Uninsured: Growing Need, Strained Resources* (Washington, D.C.: Kaiser Commission on Medicaid and the Uninsured, 2005), www.kff.org/uninsured/upload/Covering-the-Uninsured-Growing-Need-Strained-Resources-Fact-Sheet.pdf.

17. Ibid.

18. Kaiser Family Foundation, *Employer Health Benefits: 2005 Summary of Findings,* www.kff.org/insurance/7315/sections/upload/7316.pdf; and Kaiser Family Foundation, "Survey Shows Private Health Insurance Premiums Rose 11.2 percent in 2004," news release, September 9, 2004, www.kff.org/insurance/chcm090904nr.cfm.

19. Kaiser Family Foundation, "Survey Shows Private Health Insurance Premiums Rose."

20. Ibid.

21. Kaiser Commission, *Covering the Uninsured.*

22. Hospital Accountability Project of the Service Employees International Union, *Why the Working Poor Pay More: A Report on the Discriminatory Pricing of healthcare,* March 2003, www.seiu.org/docUploads/Discriminatory_Pricing__why_working_poor_pay_more.pdf.

23. The World Health Organization reports that in 2002, the United States government paid for 44.9 percent of health expenses in the United States. The United States is tied for 131st place with Mexico and Ethiopia for the amount of health expenses paid by the government. Two-thirds of the countries in the World Health Organization pay more of their people's health costs than the United States does. In the World Health Organization membership of 191 countries, seventy-nine of them pay at least 65 percent of their people's health expenses. One hundred and seventeen of them pay at least half of their people's health expenses. WHO, *World Health Report 2005,* www.who.int/whr/2005/annex/annexe5_en.pdf.

24. Ibid., www.who.int/whr/2005/annex/annexe6_en.pdf.

25. Ibid. (same infant mortality rate: www.who.int/whr/2005/annex/annexe2a_en.pdf; spending:www.who.int/whr/2005/annex/annexe6_en. pdf).

26. Ibid., www.who.int/whr/2005/annex/annexe5_en.pdf, 199.

27. Ibid.

28. Francesca Colombo and Nicole Tapay, "Private Health Insurance in OECD Countries: The Benefits and Costs for Individuals and Health Systems" (working paper, Organisation for Economic Co-operation and Development,

Paris, 2004), www.oecd.org/dataoecd/34/56/33698043.pdf; and Steffie Wool-handler et al., "Costs of healthcare Administration in the United States and Canada," *New England Journal of Medicine* 349, no. 8 (2003).

29. American Federation of Labor and Congress of Industrial Organizations, "Executive Paywatch Database," www.aflcio.org/corporatewatch/pay-watch/ceou/database.cfm?tkr=AET&pg=1.

30. Woolhandler et al., "Costs of healthcare Administration."

31. Morton Mintz, "Single-Payer: Good for Business," *The Nation,* November 15, 2004, www.thenation.com/doc/20041115/mintz.

32. Woolhandler et al., "healthcare Administration in the United States and Canada: Micromanagement, Macro Costs," *International Journal of Health Services* 34, no. 1 (2004), www.pnhp.org/news/IJHS_US_v_Canada _Paper.pdf.

33. Steve Erwin, "Toyota to build 100,000 vehicles per year in Woodstock, Ontario, starting 2008," CBC News, www.cbc.ca/cp/business/050630/ b0630102.html.

34. Mintz, "Single-Payer: Good for Business."

35. The Kaiser Family Foundation, "Health Insurance Coverage of Children 0–18, States (2003–2004), U.S. (2004)," State Health Facts, www.statehealth-facts.org/cgi-bin/healthfacts.cgi?action=compare&category=Health+Cov-erage+%26+Uninsured&subcategory=Health+Insurance+Status&topic=C hildren+%280%2d18%29 (accessed January 2006).

36. Center for Women's Business Research, *A Compendium of National Statistics on Women-Owned Businesses in the U.S., report prepared for.the National Women's Business Council, September 2001, www.nwbc.gov/documents/com-pendium.pdf.*

6. Excellent Childcare Endnotes:

1. Karen Schulman, *Key Facts: Essential Information about childcare, Early Educa-tion and School-Age Care* (Children's Defense Fund, 2003), 8

2. Karen Schulman, *Key Facts,* 3.

3. Julia Overturf Johnson, *Who's Minding the Kids? childcare Arrangements: Winter 2002,* Current Population Reports, U.S. Census Bureau, Washington, D.C., 2005.

4. "While no national data are available, a study of childcare centers in California revealed that the average turnover rate between 1999 and 2000 was 30 percent

for all teaching staff. Over half (56 percent) of these centers that reported turnover in 1999 had not succeeded in replacing the staff they had lost. Three-quarters (76 percent) of the teaching staff employed in the childcare centers studied in 1996 and 82 percent of those working in programs in 1994 were no longer working in those childcare centers in 2000," wrote Karen Schulman, National Women's Law Center, in a December 16, 2005 e-mail to the author, sourcing Marcy Whitebook et al., *Then and Now: Changes in childcare Staffing, 1994–2000* (Washington, D.C.: Center for the childcare Workforce, 2001).

5. Jody Heymann et al., *The Work, Family, and Equity Index: Where Does the United States Stand Globally?* (Boston: Project on Global Working Families, 2004), 2.

6. Children's Defense Fund calculations, based on data from the U.S. Census Bureau, Current Population Survey Annual Demographic Supplement, Detailed Income Tables, "Table FINC-03. Presence of Related Children Under 18 Years Old—All Families, by Total Money Income in 2001, Type of Family Work Experience in 2001, Race and Hispanic Origin of Reference Person," ferret.bls.census.gov/macro/032002/faminc/new03_000.htm.

7. Karen Schulman, *Key Facts,* 7.

8. Heymann et al., *The Work, Family, and Equity Index,* 2.

9. Ibid., 44.

10. Karen Schulman, *Key Facts,* 4.

11. Karen Schulman, *Key Facts,* 4.

12. Karen Schulman, *Key Facts,* 5.

13. Raquel Bernal and Michael P. Keane, "Maternal Time, childcare and Child Cognitive Development: The Case of Single Mothers," 2005, eswc2005.econ.ucl.ac.uk/papers/ESWC/2005/1405/Bernal_Keane_Material%20Time_01_2005.pdf; and Reuters, "Childcare Choices Impact Kids' Achievement," MSNBC, August 2, 2005, msnbc.msn.com/id/9042555/.

14. Bureau of Labor Statistics, "Table 1. National Employment and Wage Data from the Occupational Employment Statistics Survey by Occupation," November 2004, www.bls.gov/news.release/ocwage.t01.htm.

15. Carnegie Corporation of New York, "Years of Promise: A Comprehensive Learning Strategy for America's Children," September 1996, www.carnegie.org/sub/pubs/execsum.html.

16. Karen Schulman, *The High Cost of childcare Puts Quality Care Out of Reach for Many Families* (Washington, D.C.: Children's Defense Fund, 2000), www.childrensdefense.org/childcare/childcare/highcost.pdf.

17. Children's Defense Fund calculations, based on data from the U.S. Census Bureau, "Table FINC-03."

18. According to Air Force Lieutenant Colonel Ellen Krenke, spokesperson for the
Department of Defense (in a May 2005 email to the author), "For FY 2004,
the appropriated fund budget was $379 million. This does not include the sup-
plemental funds as they are not meant for or used for regular operations. The
number of children served in our child development program according to our
2004 annual report from the Services and Defense Logistics Agency is 207,211."

19. National Women's Law Center, "Military childcare Continues to Serve as
Model for the Country, NWLC Report Shows," news release, August 10,
2005, www.nwlc.org/details.cfm?id=2357&section=newsroom.

20. Ibid.

21. Schulman, *The High Cost of Childcare.*

22. "The official poverty rate in 2003 was 12.5 percent, up from 12.1 percent in
2002. In 2003, 35.9 million people were in poverty, up 1.3 million from 2002.
From 2000 both the poverty number and rate have risen for three consecu-
tive years, from 31.6 million and 11.3 percent in 2000, to 35.9 million and
12.5 percent in 2003." U.S. Census Bureau, "People: Poverty,"
factfinder.census.gov/jsp/saff/SAFFInfo.jsp?_pageId=tp8_poverty.

23. National Women's Law Center, "Military childcare Continues to Serve as
Model."

24. Barbara Sporcic, child and youth services coordinator at Fort Lewis in Washington State, interview with the author, May 19, 2005.

25. National Women's Law Center, "Military childcare Continues to Serve as
Model."

26. Ibid.

27. Ibid.

28. Sporcic, interview with the author, May 19, 2005.

29. Clive Belfield and Dennis Winters, *An Economic Analysis of Four-Year-Old
Kindergarten in Wisconsin.* (Trust for Early Education, 2004) www.pre
know.org/documents/WIEconImpactReport_Sept2005.pdf.

30. Karen Schulman *Key Facts,* 8; J. Lee Kreader et al., *Scant Increases After Welfare Reform: Regulated childcare Supply in Illinois and Maryland, 1996–1998*
(New York: Columbia University, National Center for Children in Poverty,
2000), www.nccp.org/media/ccr00c-text.pdf.

31. Karen Schulman,*Key Facts,* 8.

32. According to Air Force Lieutenant Colonel Ellen Krenke, spokesperson for
the Department of Defense (in a May 2005 email to the author), "For FY
2004, the appropriated fund budget was $379 million. This does not include
the supplemental funds as they are not meant for or used for regular operations. The number of children served in our child development program

according to our 2004 annual report from the Services and Defense Logistics Agency is 207,211."

33. Schulman, *The High Cost of childcare.*

34. Bureau of Labor Statistics, "National Employment and Wage Data."

35. Belfield and Winters, *An Economic Analysis of Four-Year-Old Kindergarten in Wisconsin.* http://www.preknow.org/documents/WIEconImpactReport_Sept2005.pdf.

36. National Association of childcare Resource and Referral Agencies, *childcare in America,* www.naccrra.org/docs/Child_Care_In_America_Facts.pdf; and Eugene Smolensky and Jennifer Appleton Gootman, eds., *Working Families and Growing Kids: Caring for Children and Adolescents* (Washington, D.C.: National Academies Press: 2003),www.nap.edu/openbook/0309087031/html/43.html.

37. Karen Schulman, *Key Facts,* 5.

7. REALISTIC AND FAIR WAGES ENDNOTES:

1. Jane Waldfogel, "Understanding the 'Family Gap' in Pay for Women with Children," *Journal of Economic Perspectives* 12, no. 1 (1998), 137–156.

2. Waldfogel, "Understanding the 'Family Gap.' "

3. Shelley Correll, "Getting a Job: Is There a Motherhood Penalty?" (paper presented at the American Sociological Association's 100th annual meeting in Philadelphia, August 15, 2005); and Daniel Aloi, "Mothers Face Disadvantages in Getting Hired, Cornell Study Says," Cornell University News Service, August 4, 2005, www.news.cornell.edu/stories/Aug05/soc.mothers.dea.html.

4. Waldfogel, "Understanding the 'Family Gap.' "

5. Ibid.

6. Heather Boushey, "No Way Out: How Prime-Age Workers Get Trapped in Minimum-Wage Jobs," *WorkingUSA: The Journal of Labor and Society* 8 (December 2005), www.cepr.net/publications/labor_markets_2005_05.pdf.

7. Waldfogel, "Understanding the 'Family Gap.' "

8. Boushey, "No Way Out."

9. Heather Boushey and John Schmitt, *Impact of Proposed Minimum-Wage Increase on Low-Income Families* (Washington, D.C.: Center for Economic and Policy Research, 2005), www.cepr.net/publications/labor_market_2005_12.pdf.

10. The Women, Infants, and Children website is at www.fns.usda.gov/wic/.

11. Boushey and Schmitt, *Impact of Proposed Minimum-Wage Increase.*

12. Economic Policy Institute, *Minimum Wage: Facts at a Glance* (Economic Policy Institute, 2005), ww.epi.org/content.cfm/issueguides_minwage_minwagefacts.

13. U.S. Department of Labor, "Minimum Wage Laws in the States: California," 2005, www.dol.gov/esa/minwage/america.htm#California.

14. DOL, "Minimum Wage," www.dol.gov/dol/topic/wages/minimumwage.htm (accessed August 2005).

15. DOL, "Minimum Wage Laws in the States," 2005, www.dol.gov/esa/minwage/america.htm.

16. DOL, "Minimum Wage Laws in the States: Florida," 2005, www.dol.gov/esa/minwage/america.htm#Florida.

17. Boushey and Schmitt, *Impact of Proposed Minimum-Wage Increase.*

18. Economic Policy Institute, *Minimum Wage: Facts at a Glance.*

19. Boushey, "No Way Out."

20. U.S. Census Bureau, "People: Income and Employment," 2005, factfinder. census.gov/jsp/saff/SAFFInfo.jsp?_pageId=tp6_income_employment.

21. The Self-Sufficiency Standard was created by Wider Opportunities for Women (WOW) and Dr. Diana Pearce, founder of the Women and Poverty Project at WOW and a professor at the University of Washington.

22. Diana Pearce with Jennifer Brooks, *The Self-Sufficiency Standard for California 2003* (Oakland, CA: National Economic Development and Law Center, 2003), www.sixstrategies.org/files/2003%20CA%20Full%20Report%20with%20Map.pdf, 10.

23. Michael Reich et al., *Living Wages and Airport Security: Preliminary Report* (Berkeley, CA: Institute for Labor and Employment, 2001), www.iir.berkeley.edu/livingwage/pdf/air_sep01.pdf, 3.

24. Ibid.

25. Ibid., 5–6.

26. Ibid., 6.

27. David Card and Alan B. Krueger, "Minimum Wages and Employment: A Case Study of the Fast-Food Industry in New Jersey and Pennsylvania," *The American Economic Review* 84, no. 4 (1994), 772–793.

28. Fiscal Policy Institute, *State Minimum Wages and Employment in Small Businesses* (New York: Fiscal Policy Institute, 2004), www.fiscalpolicy.org/minimumwageandsmallbusiness.pdf.

29. Ibid., 16.

30. Jared Bernstein et al., *The Minimum Wage Increase: A Working Woman's Issue* (Economic Policy Institute, 1999), www.epinet.org/content.cfm/issue-briefs_ib133.

31. U.S. Census Bureau, "Table H1. Percent Childless and Births per 1,000 Women in the Last Year: Selected Years, 1976 to Present, 2001," www.census.gov/population/socdemo/fertility/tabH1.pdf.

32. U.S. Census Bureau, "People: Income and Employment."

33. In 1980, mothers earned 56 percent of men's salaries, while non-mothers earned 66 percent (a 10 percent mommy wage gap). But by 1991, non-mothers' earnings rocketed to 90.1 percent, while mothers earned only 72.6 percent (an increased 17.5 percent mommy wage gap). Waldfogel, "Understanding the 'Family Gap.' "

34. AFL-CIO, "What's Wrong with CEO Pay (2004)," www.aflcio.org/corporate america/paywatch/retirementsecurity/case_walmart.cfm (accessed August 2005).

35. Stephen Bezruchka, "The (Bigger) Picture of Health," in John de Graaf, ed., *Take Back Your Time: Fighting Overwork and Time Poverty in America* (San Francisco: Berrett-Koehler Publishers, 2003).

36. Paul Krugman, "Always Low Wages. Always." *New York Times*, May 13, 2005, www.commondreams.org/views05/0513-26.htm.

37. Ibid.

38. Correll, "Getting a Job"; and Aloi, "Mothers Face Disadvantages."

8. AS MOTHERS GO, SO GOES THE COUNTRY ENDNOTE

1. National Conference of State Legislatures, "Unlawful Discrimination in Employment Laws," July 2004, www.ncsl.org/programs/employ/empdisc.htm.